HOME REPAIR AND IMPROVEMENT

REPAIRING FURNITURE

TIME®
LIFE
BOOKS

OTHER PUBLICATIONS:

DO IT YOURSELF
The Time-Life Complete Gardener
Home Repair and Improvement
The Art of Woodworking
Fix It Yourself

COOKING
Weight Watchers® Smart Choice Recipe Collection
Great Taste/Low Fat
Williams-Sonoma Kitchen Library

HISTORY
The American Story
Voices of the Civil War
The American Indians
Lost Civilizations
Mysteries of the Unknown
Time Frame
The Civil War
Cultural Atlas

TIME-LIFE KIDS
Family Time Bible Stories
Library of First Questions and Answers
A Child's First Library of Learning
I Love Math
Nature Company Discoveries
Understanding Science & Nature

SCIENCE/NATURE
Voyage Through the Universe

For information on and a full description
of any of the Time-Life Books series listed above,
please call 1-800-621-7026 or write:

Reader Information
Time-Life Customer Service
P.O. Box C-32068
Richmond Virginia 23261-2068

HOME REPAIR AND IMPROVEMENT

REPAIRING FURNITURE

BY THE EDITORS OF TIME-LIFE BOOKS, ALEXANDRIA, VIRGINIA

The Consultants

Jon Arno, a wood technologist residing in Michigan where he works for a family lumber business, is known for his skills in furniture design and cabinetmaking. Mr. Arno has written extensively on the properties and use of wood and is the author of *The Woodworkers Visual Handbook* and a frequent contributor to *Fine Woodworking* magazine. He also conducts seminars on wood identification and early American furniture design.

Steve Cone, the owner and operator of Cone Upholstery in St. Paul, Minnesota, has more than three decades of experience in the upholstery industry. He designed and implemented the Upholstery program at Century College in Minnesota. Mr. Cone writes a monthly column for the *Upholstery Journal* and has conducted upholstery workshops throughout North America.

Louina Legresley is president of St. Urbain Upholstery. Ms. Legresley apprenticed under a German-trained craftsman and subsequently taught upholstery techniques at St. Columba House in Montreal, Quebec.

Paul McGoldrick owns and operates Pianoforte, a piano restoration business established in Montreal, Quebec, in 1978. Mr. McGoldrick, who trained as a cabinetmaker, specializes in fine wood finishes and the maintenance and preparation of concert pianos.

K.C. Parkinson, owner and operator of Connecticut Cane and Reed Co. in Manchester, Connecticut, previously owned a furniture restoration business. He is accomplished in furniture restoration and is an expert chair-seat weaver. Mr. Parkinson has contributed to numerous publications and is the co-publisher of the magazine *Shakers World* .

CONTENTS

Basic Joinery Repairs

Most well-made furniture is held together by joints that are reinforced by glue or hardware. With ordinary wear and tear, these joints can work loose—chairs and tables wobble, bed frames break, and drawers come apart. Restoring a piece of furniture to usefulness is often simply a matter of gently separating the parts, then regluing or refastening them.

Gluing a split mortise →

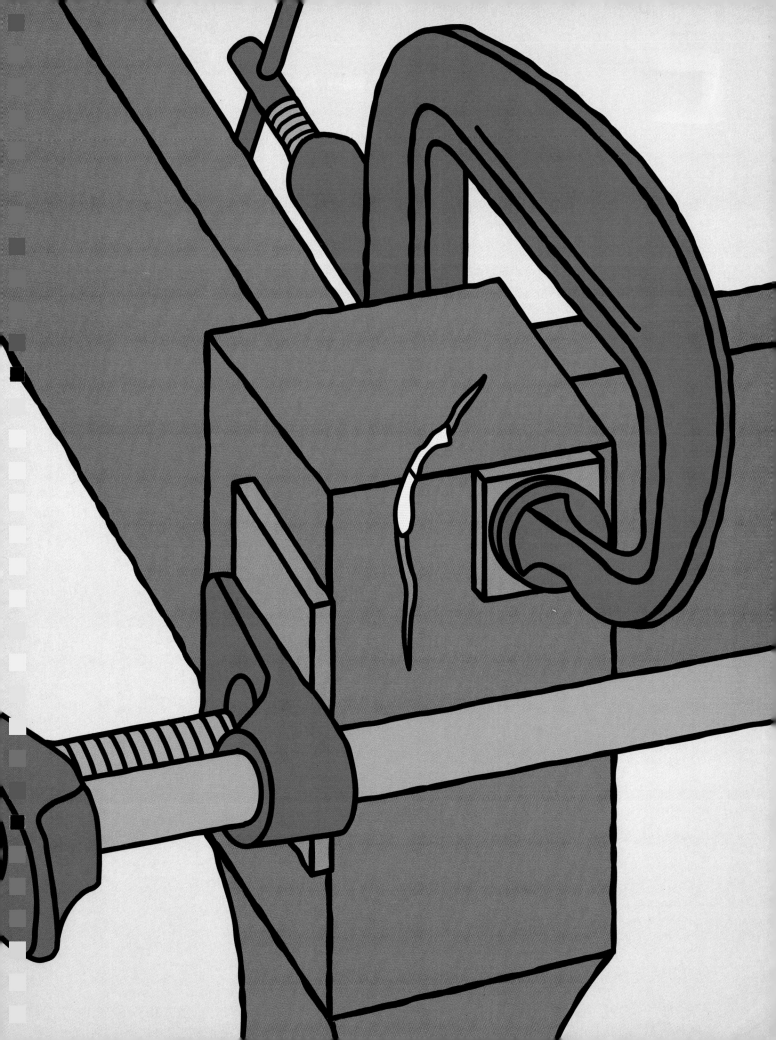

Strengthening Chair Joints

The typical chair has mortise-and-tenon joints, in which a round or square end on one part fits into a corresponding mortise, or socket, in a second part. These joints often loosen or separate because of the pressure exerted on them.

If a chair has only one weak joint, it can generally be tightened and reglued without taking the chair apart *(pages 10-13)*. When more than one joint has loosened, it is best to disassemble the chair *(pages 13-14)*; but break it down into as few subassemblies as possible to avoid further damage. Once the joints are accessible, they can be reinforced with shims or wedges *(pages 15-17)* before the chair is reassembled *(pages 18-19)*.

 TOOLS

	Pliers	Web clamps	Coping saw
Shop knife	Electric drill	Socket wrench	Dovetail saw
Hammer	Glue injector	Circular saw	Awl
Nail set	Rubber mallet	Handsaw	Screwdriver
	Wood chisel	Sanding block	Bar clamps

 **MATERIALS**   Sandpaper
(medium grade)

Wood glue   Cork
Cheesecloth   Furniture veneer
Dowel   Wax paper
Hardwood stock   Replacement
  for wedges   screws

 SAFETY TIPS

Protect your eyes with goggles when hammering or when using power tools.

A platform chair.

Generally, the legs of a platform chair fit into mortises on the bottom of the seat and are reinforced with horizontal members called stretchers. In the back assembly, stiles support each end of a top rail, and spindles fill in between. The mortise-and-tenon joints of platform chairs and frame chairs *(right)* are sometimes made with the tenon cut smaller than the member, forming a shoulder that abuts the adjoining piece.

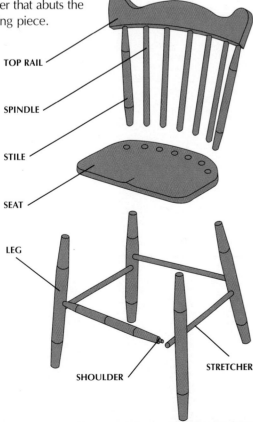

TOP RAIL
SPINDLE
STILE
SEAT
LEG
SHOULDER
STRETCHER

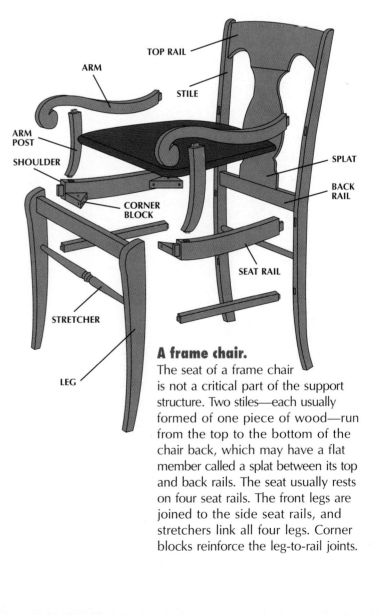

TOP RAIL
ARM
STILE
ARM POST
SHOULDER
SPLAT
BACK RAIL
CORNER BLOCK
SEAT RAIL
STRETCHER
LEG

A frame chair.

The seat of a frame chair is not a critical part of the support structure. Two stiles—each usually formed of one piece of wood—run from the top to the bottom of the chair back, which may have a flat member called a splat between its top and back rails. The seat usually rests on four seat rails. The front legs are joined to the side seat rails, and stretchers link all four legs. Corner blocks reinforce the leg-to-rail joints.

SELECTING AND USING FURNITURE GLUES

Making a strong bond.

A proper glue joint consists of a thin film of glue between layers of glue-impregnated wood fiber *(right)*. The strength of a glued joint is so great that the surrounding wood will usually break before the glue or the glue-soaked fibers do.

◆ To ensure a strong joint, clean old glue, dirt, and finish from the mating surfaces. Roughen smooth wood by scoring the surface with a knife. Allow moist wood to dry. Shape the joint so the fit is tight, leaving no gaps.

◆ Apply a thin layer of glue to each surface; on end grain, which is more absorbent, apply a slightly thicker layer.

◆ Clamp the joint, applying enough pressure to extrude a thin glue bead from the joint, but not enough to force out all the glue. Clean off the extruded adhesive with a damp cloth, then with a dry one; check immediately for correct alignment and adjust the clamping pressure, if necessary.

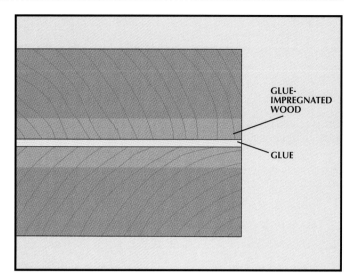

GLUE-IMPREGNATED WOOD

GLUE

CHOOSING THE RIGHT GLUE FOR THE JOB

Glue type	Open time	Clamping time	Curing time	Characteristics
Polyvinyl acetate (white glue)	3-5 min.	45 min. to 1 hr.	24-72 hrs.	Ready to use. Apply to both surfaces unless the joint is tight. Not moisture-resistant. Does not sand well.
Aliphatic resin (yellow glue)	5 min.	30 min. to 1 hr.	24 hrs.	Similar to white glue but sands easier, is slightly stronger, and dribbles less. Somewhat moisture-resistant. Only weatherproof varieties should be used on outdoor furniture.
Hide glue	10 min.	2-3 hrs.	24 hrs.	Applied at temperatures near 70°F; one type needs to be heated. Bond is reversible with moisture and heat. Sands well.
Urea-formaldehyde (plastic-resin glue)	10-30 min.	8 hrs.	24 hrs.	Very strong and weatherproof. Comes as a powder to be mixed with water. Glue is applied to both surfaces at temperatures above 70°F. Sands well.
Resorcinol	10 min.	8 hrs.	10-12 hrs.	Similar to plastic resin but stronger and more weatherproof. Comes as a liquid to be mixed with a powder catalyst. Not viscous enough to fill gaps well, so joints must fit perfectly.

Comparing glues.

The chart above lists the glues most favored for furniture repair. Those with a longer open time—the length of time before they begin to dry—give you more opportunity to adjust the alignment of a joint; however, these glues generally have to be kept clamped longer. Although clamps can be removed after the time indicated in the chart, do not disturb the joint until the glue has completely cured. Both white and yellow glue are easy to work with and either is acceptable for indoor furniture. The popular choice of professionals, hide glue, was used in most antiques. Joints made with hide glue can be separated easily with moisture and heat *(page 14)*. For outdoor furniture, choose one of the weatherproof types—urea-formaldehyde, resorcinol, or water-resistant yellow glue.

RELEASING LOCKED JOINTS

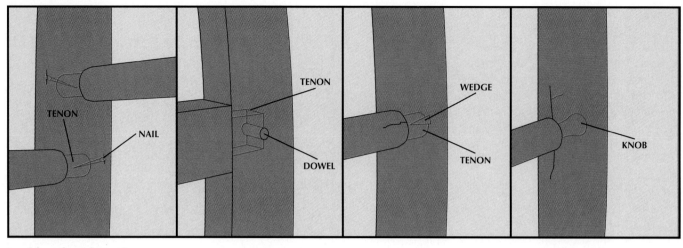

TENON
NAIL

TENON
DOWEL

TENON
WEDGE
TENON

WEDGE
KNOB

Looking for obstacles.

Before separating a joint, check for hidden fasteners. A dimple near the joint may indicate a small nail securing the end of the tenon *(left)*. Drive the nail partway through with a nail set; when the tip appears, extract the nail with pliers.

Where a dowel pins a mortise-and-tenon joint together *(left center)*, try tapping it out with a hammer and a smaller dowel. If it is glued in place, drill the dowel out with a drill bit of a slightly smaller diameter.

Hairline cracks on the sides of a tenon at the point where it emerges from its socket generally mean that the tenon has been wedged *(right center)*. Cracks above and below a tenon where it enters an oval stile or rail are typical of an older style "shrink joint" *(right)*, in which a knobbed end of dry wood is fitted into a socket while the wood of the socketed member is still wet or "green." The socket then shrinks around the knob as it dries. Disassembling either a wedged or shrink joint can split the wood; instead, repair these joints by injecting glue from the outside *(opposite)*.

ATTACHING A ROUND TENON

1. Cleaning and regluing the joint.

◆ Gently separate the joint. If necessary tap the pieces with a rubber mallet—to avoid marring the wood use a white rubber mallet, or protect the wood with a wood scrap.
◆ Scrape glue off the tenon with a shop knife and out of the mortise with a small chisel or gouge, taking care to remove as little wood as possible.
◆ Tap the joint together to see if it is tight, then pull it apart again. If the joint is loose, build it up by wrapping the tenon with a strip of cheesecloth soaked in glue.
◆ Apply a thin coat of wood glue to the tenon and mortise *(right)*.
◆ Tap the joint back together.

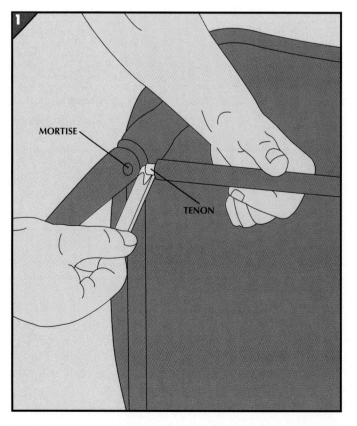

MORTISE
TENON

2. Clamping the piece.
◆ Set the chair upright on a flat surface.
◆ Wrap a web clamp around the pair of affected legs and tighten the clamp just enough to pull the joint together and seat the tenon completely *(left)*.

TRICKS OF THE TRADE

Injecting Glue

Damaged joints that can't be separated can be reglued using a syringe-type glue injector filled with wood glue. If the joint can be pulled apart slightly, inject adhesive directly into the mortise. Smear glue over the exposed part of the tenon and press the joint back together again. If you can't separate the joint, drill a hole slightly larger than the tip of the injector into the back of the mortise. Push the tip of the injector into the hole and squeeze the plunger until glue appears all around the tenon *(right)*. You may have to drill and inject glue into a second hole if it is difficult to get glue into the first one or if the glue comes out on only one side of the mortise. Conceal the hole with wood filler.

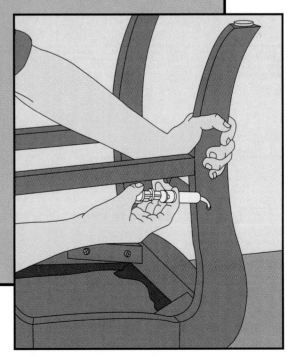

ADDING WEDGES

1. Making wedges.
To fill the gaps around a loose tenon, cut wedges from a piece of hardwood: Align a circular saw blade $\frac{1}{4}$ inch from the edge of the board and make an angled cut with the grain of the wood, forming 3-inch-long wedges that taper gradually to a sharp point *(right)*. For very loose joints, prepare wedges for all four sides; otherwise, make one wedge per joint. For economical use of wood, alternate angled cuts with straight cuts that square off the board.

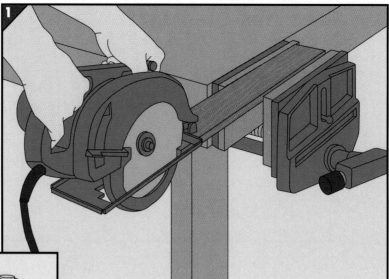

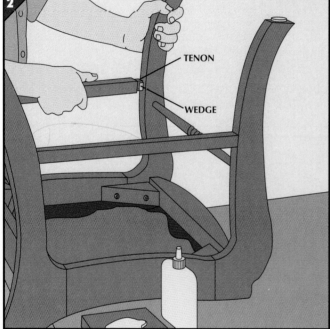

TENON

WEDGE

2. Wedging the tenon.
◆ Check for obstacles *(page 10)*. If the tenon is pinned with a dowel, take the appropriate steps to deal with it *(below, Step 1)*. If the joint is not pinned, gently pull it apart.
◆ Trim the wedges to fit between the tenon and mortise.
◆ With a glue injector, force wood glue into the mortise. Apply glue to the exposed part of the tenon and coat both sides of each wedge.
◆ Insert wedges into the gaps around the tenon, and press the joint together. On a shouldered tenon, the shoulders will drive the wedges into place *(left)*; on a tenon with no shoulder, drive in the wedges with a mallet and a small wood block.
◆ Clamp the joint *(page 11, Step 2)*.

DEALING WITH A DOWEL PIN

1. Drilling out a dowel pin.
If a square tenon pinned with a dowel has no shoulder, do not drill out the dowel; instead, make wedges *(above, Step 1)* and, without pulling the joint apart, glue them around the tenon *(above, Step 2)*.

For a shouldered tenon pinned with a dowel, fit a drill with a bit the same diameter as the dowel you plan to insert. Centering the bit on the dowel, drill the dowel out. Wedge the tenon *(above, Step 2)*.

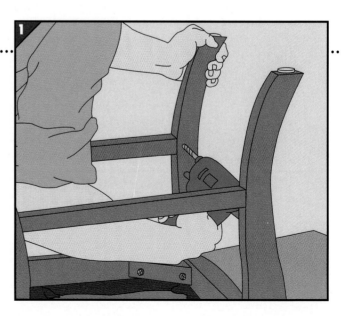

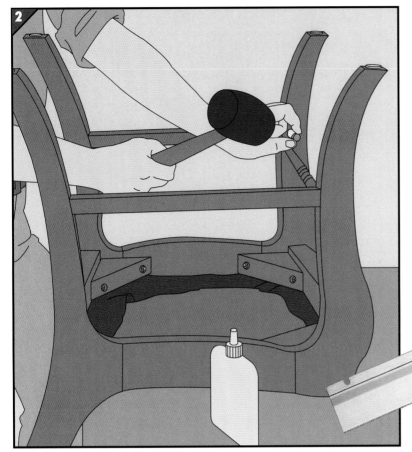

2. Pinning the joint.

◆ Cut a new dowel slightly longer than the depth of the hole. Bevel one end of it to make it easier to insert.

◆ Redrill the dowel hole to clear out parts of wedges that may obstruct it.

◆ Spread glue in the hole and on the dowel, and tap the pin into the hole with a mallet *(left)*.

◆ Let the glue dry, then, with medium-grade sandpaper, sand the protruding end of the dowel flush with the surrounding surface. A flush-cutting saw can be used instead of sandpaper *(photograph)*.

◆ Finish the end of the dowel to match the rest of the chair *(pages 73-81)*.

TAKING A CHAIR APART

A platform chair.

◆ Set the chair on its side with the seat in a vise, protecting the wood with cloth.

◆ To release the back assembly, grasp each stile and spindle in turn and tap on the seat with a mallet. Protect the chair with a block of wood faced with cork, or use a white rubber mallet.

◆ Turn the chair upside down and tap on the bottom of the seat while pulling on each leg in turn to release the leg assembly *(right)*.

◆ Take apart the subassemblies if necessary by separating the joints *(page 10)*.

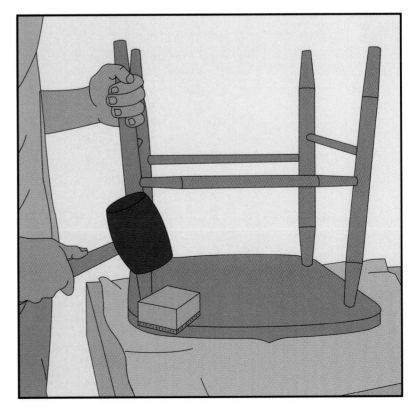

A frame chair.

Frame chairs rarely need to be taken apart completely; usually only a stretcher needs to be removed. If the chair has no corner blocks, do not use this method —the seat-rail joints may fail; knock the stretchers loose with a mallet.

◆ Set the chair upside down.

◆ Make a lever by cutting a piece of wood slightly longer than the span between the pair of legs. Cut the piece in half and, with a coping saw, trim one end of each piece so it is cupped; cut a V and an inverted V in the other ends.

◆ Position the lever so the cupped ends rest on the legs just above the stretcher; place cloth between the ends and the chair to protect the finish.

◆ Join the ends with the V cuts, and push down slowly and steadily on the lever to spread the joint apart *(right)*. Instead of making a lever, you can reverse the jaws of a quick clamp *(photograph)* and spread the jaws to loosen the joints.

◆ Remove the stretcher.

LEVER

STRETCHER

CORNER BLOCK

SEAT RAIL

TRICKS OF THE TRADE

Separating Stubborn Joints

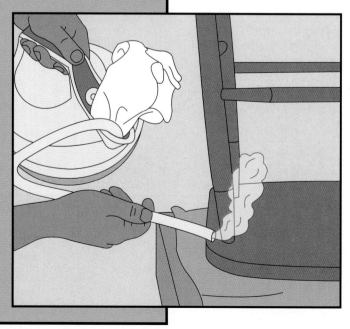

The joints in older furniture may be held fast with hide glue, and can be released with steam. Fill an electric kettle with water, place a rubber hose in the spout, stuff a rag around it, and plug in the kettle. Once steam begins to come out of the hose, hold the end against the joint for a few minutes *(right)*. Pull the joint apart.

If the joint doesn't come apart, it has likely been fastened with a modern glue. Some glues can be softened by injecting methyl alcohol into the joint with a syringe; avoid spreading the solution beyond the joint as it can damage the finish. Allow it to soak in for a few minutes and then separate the joint.

1. Cleaning off old glue.

For a disassembled chair, rather than simply regluing a round tenon (page 10), you can achieve a tighter joint by adding a wedge.

◆ Disassemble the joint (pages 13-14).

◆ Scrape old glue from the tenoned end with a shop knife, holding the blade almost perpendicular to the wood but tilted slightly forward to drag across the surface. Apply as much force as needed to remove glue without digging into the wood.

◆ Wrap the mortised piece in cloth to protect its finish and clamp it in a vise, mortise up. Scrape out old glue with a $\frac{1}{4}$-inch chisel, taking care not to remove any wood (right). Then enlarge the bottom of the socket slightly to make room for the wedged tenon.

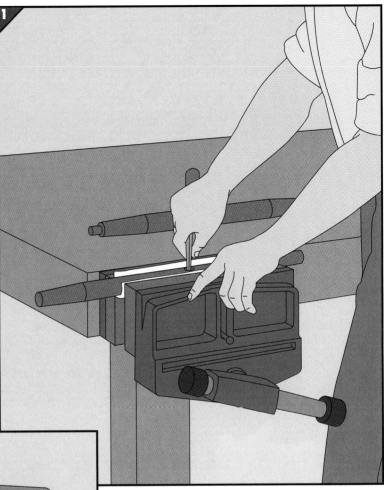

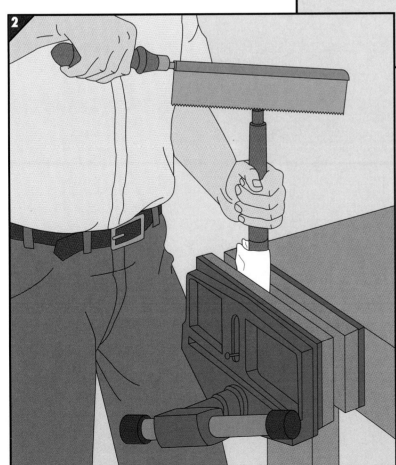

2. Cutting a kerf in the tenon.

With a dovetail saw or a small backsaw, cut a kerf in the end of the tenon (left), stopping just short of the shoulder. If the piece has no shoulder, stop cutting at the point where the tenon will be visible once the joint is assembled.

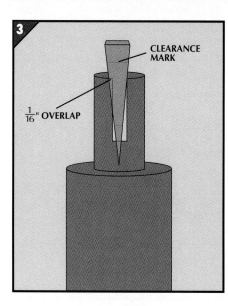

CLEARANCE MARK

$\frac{1}{16}$" OVERLAP

3. Wedging the tenon.
◆ Cut a hardwood wedge *(page 12, Step 1, top).*
◆ Measure the depth of the mortise and the length of the tenon to find the clearance between the end of the tenon and the bottom of the mortise.
◆ Hold the wedge alongside the kerf, tapered end down, so the thickness of the wedge at the top of the tenon is $\frac{1}{16}$ inch greater than the width of the kerf, then mark the thick end of the wedge beyond the end of the tenon by a distance equal to the clearance depth; mark the tapered end just short of the bottom of the kerf *(left). (For the sake of clarity, the kerf illustrated here is wider than one made with a dovetail saw.)*
◆ Cut the wedge at the two marks.
◆ Bind the wedge to the tenon with a rubber band until you are ready to glue the chair back together. When you tap the joint in place, the top of the wedge will contact the bottom of the mortise and spread out the tenon.

MENDING A BREAK

1. Drilling a dowel hole.
◆ Disassemble the joint *(pages 13-14).*
◆ Saw off the broken end of the tenon and, with medium-grade sandpaper, sand it flush with the shoulder.
◆ Dimple the center of the tenoned piece with an awl.
◆ Wrap the piece in cloth and clamp it in a vise.

◆ Fit a drill with a bit of the same diameter as the mortise in the mating piece. Aligning the bit at the angle of the old tenon—usually parallel to the chair part—drill a hole to the depth of the mortise.
◆ Bevel a dowel to fit into the hole, seat it in fully, and trim it so the part that projects is three-quarters the depth of the mortise in the mating piece.

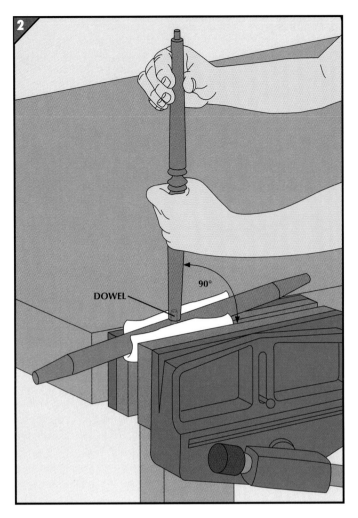

2. Checking the alignment.

◆ Saw, sand, and drill out any portion of the broken tenon left in the mortise, as in Step 1.

◆ Clamp the mortised chair part in the vise so the walls of the mortise are perpendicular to the top of the vise. Fit the joint together *(left)*. If the tenoned piece does not form close to a right angle with the top of the vise, glue the dowel into it, trim the dowel flush, and rebore the hole as in Step 1. Otherwise apply wood glue to both ends of the dowel and assemble the joint.

SHIMMING A SQUARE TENON

Applying veneer shims.

◆ Disassemble the joint *(pages 13-14)*.

◆ Cut pieces of furniture veneer slightly larger than the sides of the tenon where there are gaps.

◆ Apply glue to the tenon and shim, and join the two *(right)*; place wax paper over the glued shim, and clamp the assembly between two wood blocks. When shimming opposite sides of a tenon, glue and clamp both sides as a unit.

◆ Remove the clamp and wax paper when the glue has dried, and trim off the excess veneer with a shop knife. Repeat for the remaining sides if necessary.

◆ Test-fit the tenon in the mortise. If you cannot seat the joint with hand pressure, pull the tenon out and sand down any shiny spots—indicating areas where it binds.

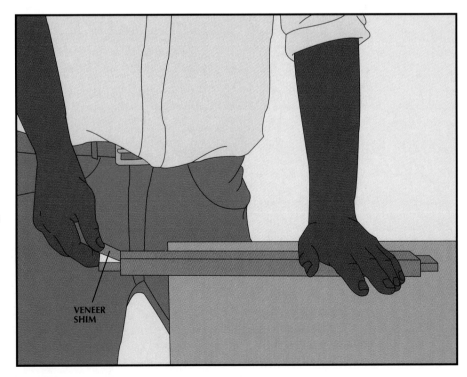

1. Assembling the legs and seat.

If the chair has been completely disassembled, test the fit by putting it together without glue and wedges:

◆ Make two H-shaped assemblies of front and back legs, each with a side stretcher.

◆ Join the two Hs with the front stretcher *(right)*, then add the back stretcher.

◆ Install the seat, then loop a web clamp around the assembly to determine the best way to fit the clamp.

◆ Disassemble the pieces and apply wood glue to the mortises, dowels, tenons, and wedges, inserting wedges into any tenons that have been prepared for them *(pages 15-16)*. Put the leg and seat assembly back together.

◆ Install the web clamp, and proceed immediately to Step 2.

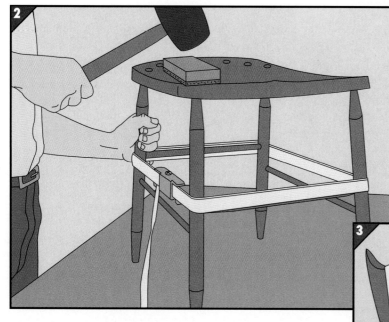

2. Leveling the chair.

◆ Place the assembly on a flat, level surface.

◆ Protecting the finish with a cork-faced block, strike the top of the seat over each leg with a mallet to firm the legs in the mortises *(left)*.

◆ Repeat for the joints between the stretchers and the legs, tightening the web clamp around the legs as you go.

◆ If the chair has arms, skip Step 3 and attach the back as described opposite.

3. Attaching the back.

◆ Without wedges or glue, fit the back assembly of the chair together, setting the stiles and spindles into their mortises.

◆ Wrap two web clamps around the back and under the seat with the clamp winches behind the back.

◆ Disassemble the back and repeat the procedure with glue, adding tenon wedges where needed.

◆ Alternately tighten the winches *(right)* and tap the top rail with a white rubber mallet until all the tenons are seated firmly in their mortises.

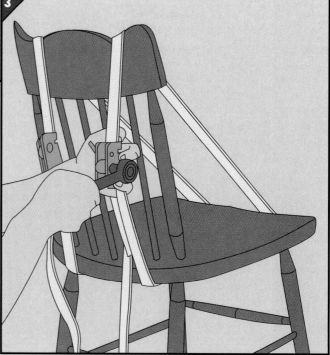

PUTTING TOGETHER AN ARMCHAIR

Assembling the parts.

◆ Follow the techniques described opposite to reassemble the chair, but in place of Step 3, assemble the back without glue: Insert the arms into the back stiles and the arm posts into the seat. Then insert the back stiles and spindles into the seat and attach the arms to their posts.

◆ Cut a temporary brace to fit exactly between the arms near their front ends.

◆ Wrap a web clamp under the seat and around the arms, near where they join the seat. With pieces of cloth protecting the arms' finish, install the brace to hold the arms apart while you tighten the clamp.

◆ Wrap a pair of web clamps around the back of the chair, passing them under the seat so the winches are positioned above the seat.

◆ Disassemble the back and arms, and put them back together with glue and, if necessary, wedges. Tighten the clamps.

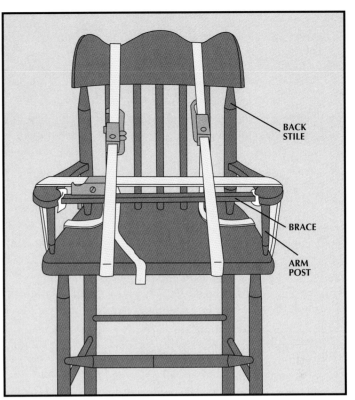

BACK STILE

BRACE

ARM POST

REBUILDING A FRAME CHAIR

Clamping the parts.

Glue up the subassemblies in the following order, test-fitting each one before applying glue. Allow the glue in each subassembly to dry before continuing.

◆ Join the back stiles and splats with the connecting rails. Lay the assembly on a flat surface and, protecting the parts with wood blocks, install a bar clamp along each rail. Adjust the clamps so the back lies flat and the two diagonal measurements are equal.

◆ Join the front legs with the front seat rail and stretcher, if any. Clamp the assembly with bar clamps.

◆ Join the front and back subassemblies with the side seat rails, and the stretchers and arm parts, if any. Install bar clamps along the side rails (left).

◆ If the chair has arms, put a brace between the ends of the arms (above) and wrap a web clamp over the front ends of the arms and under the seat. Place another web clamp horizontally around the ends of the arms and the back.

◆ Place the chair on a flat, level surface. Tap adjoining pieces together with a mallet and tighten the clamps until all of the joints are firm and the legs contact the surface evenly.

◆ Install the corner blocks with glue and screws, and once the glue has dried, screw the seat back on.

SIDE SEAT RAIL

Cures for Ailing Tables

Even the sturdiest table can eventually succumb to wear and tear. The joints at the tops of the legs are often the first to loosen or break. Working parts such as drop leaves or extensions also frequently require attention.

Stabilizing Joints: In typical table construction, the top is attached to an apron (a rectangular frame of narrow boards joined to the tops of the legs) or to corner blocks (triangular wood blocks fastened to the legs). When the hardware securing the top loosens, remove it *(below and opposite)* and replace the screws with slightly larger-diameter ones. Loose leg-to-apron joints *(opposite)* can generally be tightened and reglued using techniques similar to those for chair joints *(pages 10-17)*. But a split or broken part in a rectangular mortise and tenon—the most common leg-to-apron joint in tables—calls for special repairs *(pages 22-23)*. Once a joint has been made fast, it can be reinforced with corner braces *(page 23)*.

Mending Moving Parts: In most cases, you can treat a balky mechanism on an extension table by cleaning and lubricating the sliding parts *(page 24)*. But for broken, bent, or missing parts, it may be necessary to replace them. A sagging drop leaf can be raised with a wood wedge *(page 24)*.

 TOOLS

Screwdriver	Crosscut saw
Wrench	Wood chisel
Electric drill	Sanding block
Glue injector	Dowel jig
C-clamps	Dowel centers
Pipe or bar clamp	Rubber mallet
	Pliers

 **MATERIALS**

Replacement wood screws and buttons	Dowels ($\frac{5}{16}$")
Wood glue	Corner plates, hanger bolts, lock washers, and wing nuts
Hardwood stock	Wood screws (No. 8)
Sandpaper (medium grade)	Silicone spray or powdered graphite

SAFETY TIPS

Protect your eyes with goggles when operating power tools.

DETACHING A TOP

Removing screws.
Turn the table upside down on a rug or pad, and remove the screws or bolts attaching the table top to the apron or corner blocks. To loosen deeply set screws, use a cabinetmaker's screwdriver—its tip's straight sides *(photograph, left)* won't mar the sides of counterbored screw holes as would the flared sides of a standard screwdriver tip *(photograph, right)*.

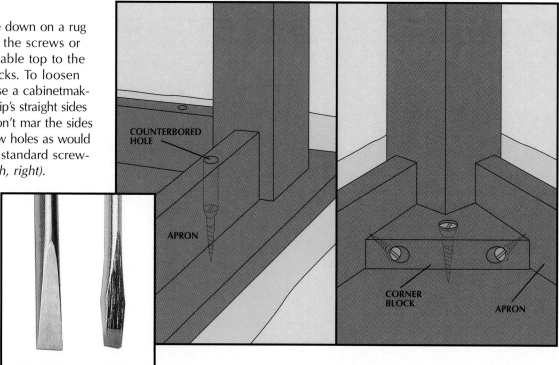

COUNTERBORED HOLE

APRON

CORNER BLOCK

APRON

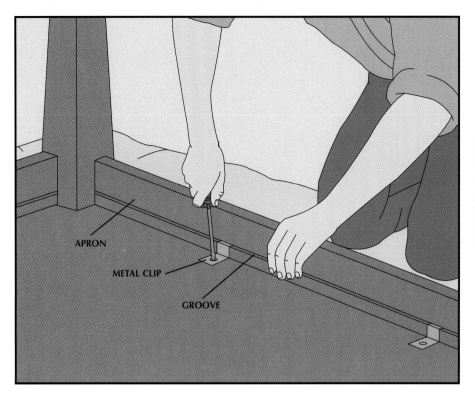

Removing clips.
For a table top held down with metal clips set in a groove in the apron, set the table upside down on a padded surface and unscrew the clips *(left)*.

APRON

METAL CLIP

GROOVE

IDENTIFYING LEG-TO-APRON JOINTS

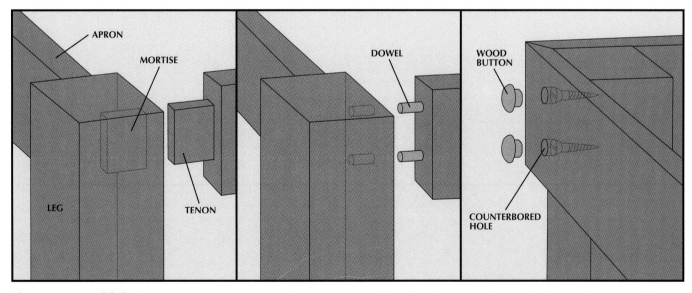

APRON

MORTISE

LEG

TENON

DOWEL

WOOD BUTTON

COUNTERBORED HOLE

Three types of joints.
A common joint is a mortise and tenon, with a tenon on the apron glued into a mortise on the leg *(above, left)*. A split mortise or broken tenon can be repaired using the techniques on pages 22 to 23.

A butt joint is usually reinforced with dowels glued into holes in the mating pieces *(above, center)*. If the dowels break, drill them out and replace them. Butt joints are sometimes reinforced by a corner plate or block *(page 23)*.

In some butt joints *(above, right)*, the apron is glued and screwed to the outer face of each leg. The screwheads are sunk below the surface of the apron in counterbored holes filled with wood plugs or buttons. If the screws pull out, drill the plugs out of the apron, remove the screws, reglue the joint, and drive in new screws of the same length but one size larger in diameter. You may have to enlarge the upper parts of the holes counterbored for the screwheads, but do not redrill the lower parts that hold the screw threads.

MENDING A SPLIT MORTISE

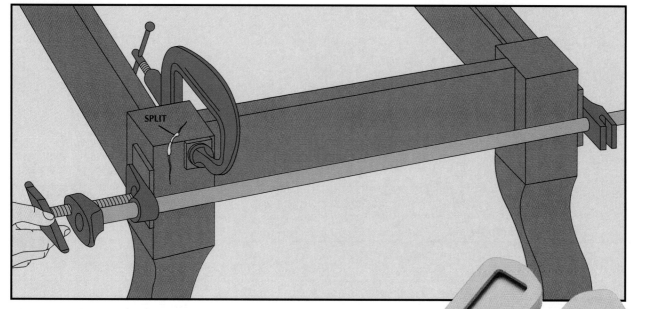

Clamping the split.

◆ With a glue injector *(page 11)*, force wood glue into the split and into the opening between the mortise and tenon.
◆ Protecting the leg with wood pads, tighten a C-clamp at the top of the leg to close the split.

◆ Install a pipe or bar clamp from the outside of the leg to the outside of an adjoining one *(above)*, again protecting the surfaces with wood blocks or special plastic pads *(photograph)*.

REPLACING A BROKEN TENON WITH DOWELS

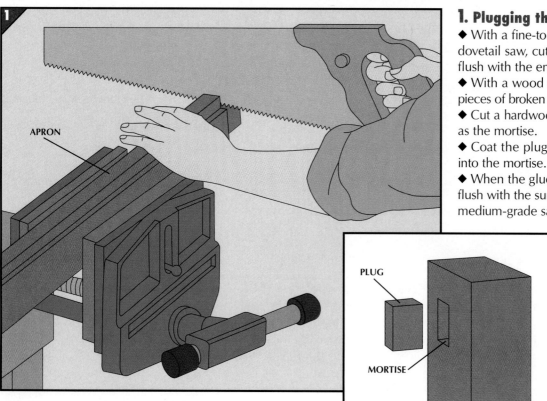

1. Plugging the mortise.

◆ With a fine-tooth crosscut saw or a dovetail saw, cut off the broken tenon flush with the end of the apron *(left)*.
◆ With a wood chisel, clear glue and pieces of broken tenon from the mortise.
◆ Cut a hardwood plug the same size as the mortise.
◆ Coat the plug with glue and tap it into the mortise.
◆ When the glue is dry, sand the plug flush with the surrounding surface using medium-grade sandpaper.

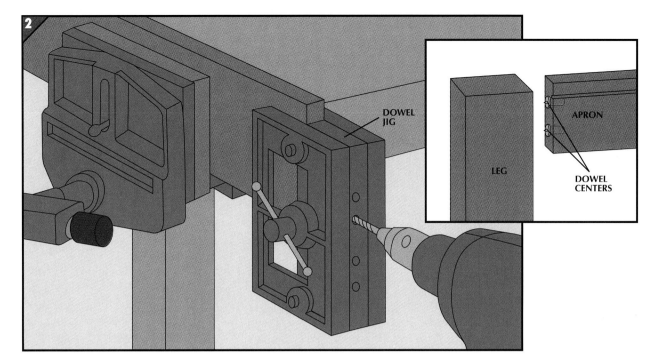

DOWEL JIG

APRON

LEG

DOWEL CENTERS

2. Making a new dowel joint.

◆ Mark two lines across the end of the apron that divide its width into thirds.

◆ Align a dowel jig with one mark and drill a $\frac{5}{16}$-inch hole $1\frac{1}{8}$ inches deep into the end of the apron *(above)*. Drill an identical hole at the other mark.

◆ Insert a dowel center—a tool for marking dowel holes—into each hole and align the apron with the leg *(inset)*. Press the centers against the leg and tap the leg of the apron with a rubber mallet so the centers indent the leg.

◆ With the dowel jig, drill a hole at each indentation identical to those in the apron.

◆ Spread a thin film of wood glue on the end of the apron and on two 2-inch-long $\frac{5}{16}$-inch dowels. Tap the dowels into the apron holes, then tap the apron to seat the dowels in the leg holes.

◆ Secure the joint with a pipe or bar clamp *(opposite)*.

REINFORCEMENT FOR A CORNER

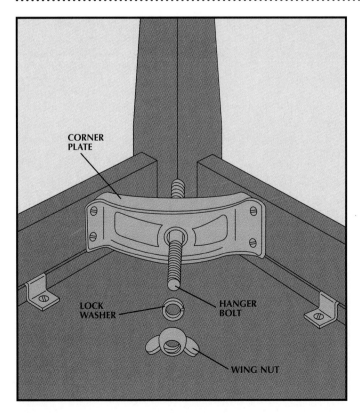

CORNER PLATE

LOCK WASHER

HANGER BOLT

WING NUT

Adding a corner plate or block.

◆ To install a metal corner plate *(left)*, first fasten it temporarily to the apron with one screw on each side.

◆ With a bit slightly smaller than the diameter of the plate's hanger bolt, drill a pilot hole into the leg through the center hole in the plate. Unscrew the plate from the apron.

◆ Unlike other fasteners, a hanger bolt has two types of threads: screw threads at one end and machine threads at the other; it also has no head. Insert the screw-thread end of the hanger bolt into the hole in the leg. Screw two nuts onto the machine-thread end and tighten them against each other with a wrench, forming a temporary head on the bolt. Turn the head to drive the screw threads completely into the leg, then remove the nuts from the bolt.

◆ Screw the plate to the apron with all four screws. Tighten a wing nut with a lock washer onto the hanger bolt.

To attach a corner block, cut a piece of hardwood in a triangle that fits the corner, with the grain running from apron to apron, and notch it to fit around the leg. Fasten the block to the aprons with No. 8 wood screws and anchor the table top to the block as illustrated on page 20.

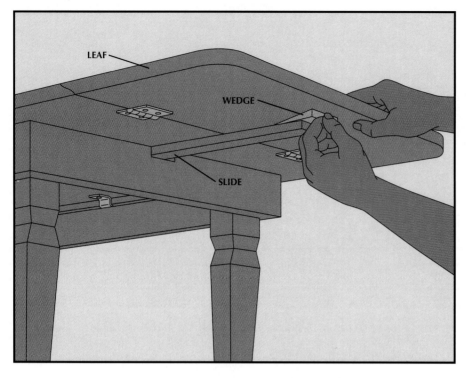

Leveling a drop leaf.

◆ Mark the underside of the leaf at the outside end of the slide when it is fully extended.

◆ With a wood chisel, scrape away any old glue or finish from the leaf in this area.

◆ Cut a thin hardwood wedge the same width as the slide.

◆ Spread wood glue on the upper face of the wedge and push it between the slide and the leaf, adjusting it until the leaf is level *(left)*.

◆ Place a weight on top of the leaf until the glue dries.

For tables that substitute the slide with a gate leg—an extra leg that folds out to support the leaf—adapt the method to glue a wedge to the underside of the leaf so the thin end points in the direction the leg swings from.

Freeing table slides.

◆ Open the table all the way; if the slide is badly worn, install a replacement *(photograph)*. Otherwise, chisel off hardened dirt and lubricant from inside the wooden tracks. Clean the sliding parts of metal tracks with a dowel.

◆ For wooden tracks, apply either a silicone spray *(right)* or beeswax to all moving parts. Sprinkle metal tracks with powdered graphite.

Where a wooden alignment pin on the edge of a leaf is broken, drill out the stub and replace it with a dowel. Glue one end of the dowel into the cleared hole and taper the other end with medium-grade sandpaper to fit loosely into the opposite hole.

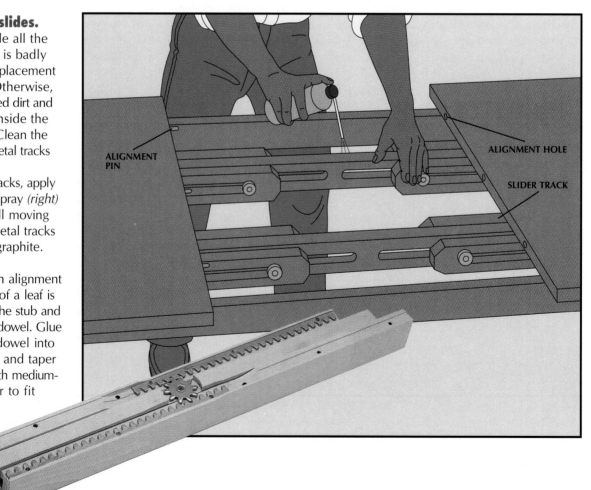

Repairing Bed Frames

Supporting the mattress and box spring of the average bed is a wood frame *(below)*. The most vulnerable spots of this structure are the joints between the side rails and bedposts: The hardware that permits the joint to be dismantled can become a source of trouble.

Knockdown Frames: On modern beds, the most common fastener hardware consists of a pair of interlocking steel plates; a plate with pins is mounted on the rail and its mating plate—either recessed or surface-mounted—goes on the bedpost. On older beds, flat metal hooks are set into the end of the side rail and enter a slot on the bedpost, where they latch over metal pins. While pin-and-hook fasteners may fail, steel-plate fasteners seldom break, but the wood around them may weaken and split. In either case, the simplest solution is to replace the fastener with a surface-mounted type *(page 26)*.

On very old beds, long bolts pass through the bedposts and extend several inches into the ends of the rails, where they are fastened by nuts embedded in the rails. The boltheads may be countersunk in the bedposts and covered with small disks. The nuts are locked in place with glue and the access holes to them in the rails are usually filled with wood plugs. These connections fail when a bolthead eats into the wood or a nut breaks away from its caul of glue, but they can easily be fixed *(page 27)*.

Other Rail Problems: The narrow ledges attached to the rails, which support slats or box springs, may sag. If so, they can be refastened and reinforced *(page 27)*. Rails that bow outward can be realigned *(page 28)*.

TOOLS

Screwdriver	C-clamp
Wood chisel	Electric drill
Handsaw	Counterbore bit
Rubber mallet	Wrench
Sanding block	Pry bar
Glue injector	Putty knife
	Bar or pipe clamp
	Carpenter's square

MATERIALS

Hardwood stock	Wood glue
Sandpaper	Epoxy glue
(medium grade)	Wood putty
Plywood ($\frac{1}{4}$")	Replacement
Wood screws	screws
($\frac{3}{4}$" No. 6)	Flat-head bolts ($\frac{3}{16}$"),
Bed-rail fastener	washers, and nuts
Bed-bolt washers	Screw eyes
	Heavy picture wire
	Turnbuckle

SAFETY TIPS

Put on goggles when operating a power tool.

Anatomy of a bed.

A bed frame is a rectangle designed to be taken apart easily when necessary. The headboard and footboard are attached to the bedposts with glued mortise-and-tenon joints, but the side rails and bedposts are fastened with knockdown hardware so the bed can be disassembled quickly. A ledge along the inside of each rail (and sometimes on the inside faces of the head- and footboard) supports box springs or the slats that hold the mattress.

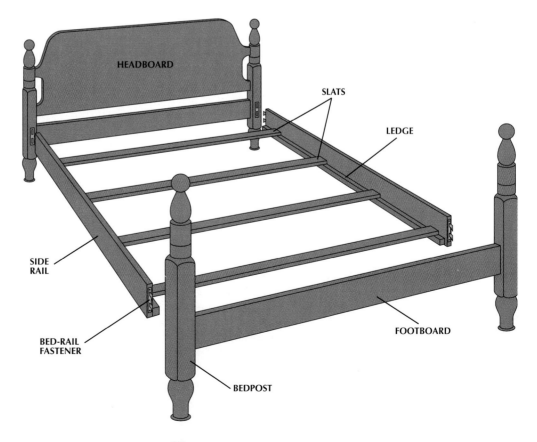

REPLACING KNOCKDOWN HARDWARE

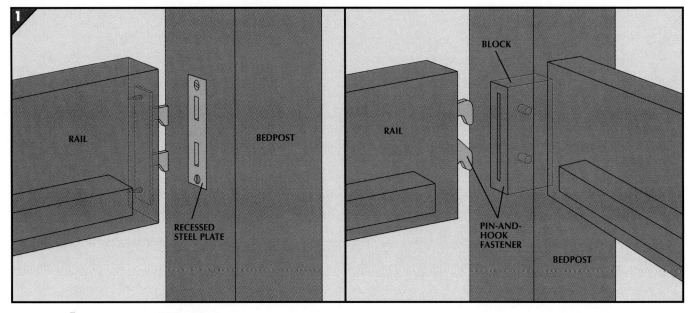

1. Removing old fasteners.

◆ Unscrew the old hardware from the rail. When the end of the rail has split, inject wood glue into the split and clamp it closed.

If a recessed metal plate is mounted on the bedpost *(above, left)*, unscrew it.

◆ For a pin-and-hook fastener set in a wood block *(above, right)*, chisel out the block.
◆ Cut a hardwood block to fit the mortise. Apply wood glue to the block and the mortise, and tap the block into the cavity with a rubber mallet.
◆ Sand the block flush with the bedpost using medium-grade sandpaper.

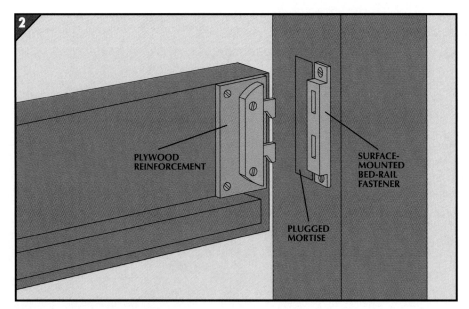

2. Installing new hardware.

◆ If the end of the rail is damaged, reinforce it with $\frac{1}{4}$-inch plywood, fastened with $\frac{3}{4}$-inch No. 6 wood screws.
◆ Interlock the two pieces of a surface-mounted bed-rail fastener.
◆ With a helper aligning the rail with the bedpost in its original position, hold the fastener against the rail and bedpost next to the plugged mortise, and mark the location of the screw holes.
◆ Drill pilot holes and screw the hardware in place.

DEALING WITH A BOLT JOINT

Tightening the joint.

To tighten a bolthead that has eaten into the wood, flip up the disk covering it and remove the bolt. Add one or two washers, then resecure the bolt in its hole *(right)*; if the bolthead protrudes above the surface, remove a washer.

◆ If the nut inside the rail spins—preventing the bolt from tightening—drill or chisel out the wood plug from the access hole *(inset)*.
◆ Unscrew the bolt and remove the loose nut, then clean the old glue from the hole with a chisel.
◆ Spread epoxy glue around the outside of the nut, keeping the threads free of glue. Replace the nut in the hole and screw in the bolt.
◆ Cut a new plug slightly longer than the access hole. Spread wood glue on the plug and in the hole, and tap the plug in with a mallet until it hits the nut.
◆ Trim and sand the plug flush with the surface.

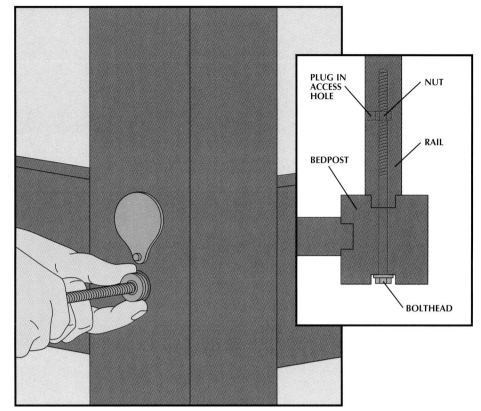

PLUG IN ACCESS HOLE

NUT

RAIL

BEDPOST

BOLTHEAD

STRENGTHENING A LOOSE OR SAGGING LEDGE

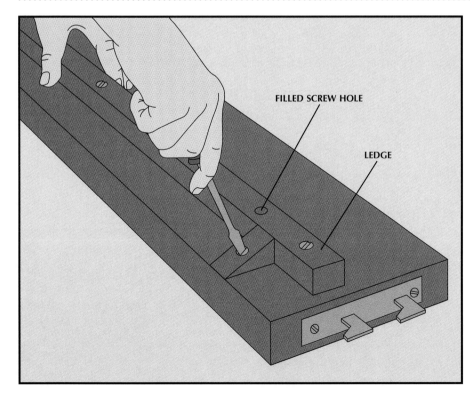

FILLED SCREW HOLE

LEDGE

Adding reinforcement.

◆ Remove the rail from the bedposts.
◆ Unscrew the ledge and gently separate it from the rail with a pry bar. (If the ledge is badly warped or cracks when you remove it, cut a new ledge from a strip of hardwood.)
◆ With a chisel, scrape old glue from the ledge and rail.
◆ Fill in the screw holes in the ledge and rail with wood putty.
◆ Every 8 inches along the ledge, mark and drill new countersunk pilot holes for screws.
◆ Attach the ledge to the rail in its original position with wood glue and screws the same size as the originals.
◆ Cut a triangular hardwood block for every 18 inches of ledge length. Drill countersunk pilot holes through the blocks, then fasten them to the rail under the ledge with glue and screws *(left)*.

Truing a slight warp.

◆ Pull the side rail into line with two bar or pipe clamps installed across the bed.

◆ Position three bed slats on the rails—one near each end and one in the middle—checking with a carpenter's square that both ends of each slat form a right angle with the rails; adjust the clamps, if necessary.

◆ Leaving a $\frac{1}{16}$-inch gap between the slat ends and the rails, drill a $\frac{3}{16}$-inch countersunk hole through each slat and into the ledge below (right).

◆ Insert $\frac{3}{16}$-inch flat-head bolts in the holes. Add washers and tighten the nuts.

◆ Set the remaining slats on the ledges without fastening them.

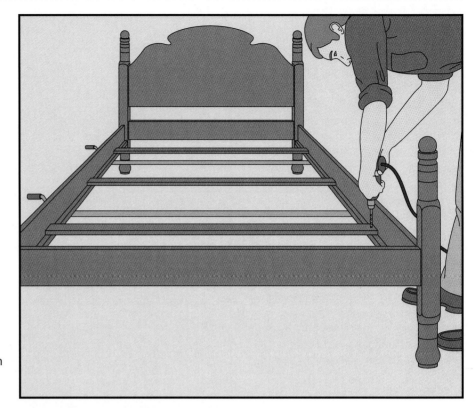

Correcting a severe bulge.

◆ Fasten screw eyes to both bedposts on the side opposite the bowed rail at ledge height. To the ledge at the center of the bowed rail, attach a third screw eye that is long enough to penetrate the ledge and half the thickness of the side rail.

◆ Fasten a length of heavy picture wire to each bedpost (inset), feed one length through the screw eye on the ledge, and join the loose ends in a turnbuckle (photograph). Insert a screwdriver in the turnbuckle's sleeve and turn it, tightening the turnbuckle and pulling the rail inward (above).

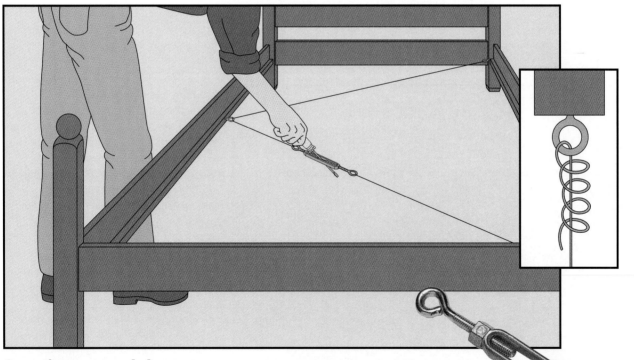

Mending Worn Cabinets

Bureaus, armoires, desks, and china cabinets all share the same types of problems: The stresses on them are different from those on chairs, tables, or beds, and it is usually their moving parts—drawers, doors, and casters—that eventually fail.

Drawers: Most older cabinets have wooden drawer guides centered between the drawer sides, and the bottoms of the sides run along the cabinet base or dust-panel frames. If a drawer sticks because a loose nail catches on a guide, simply drive the nail back in. A sagging drawer bottom can be turned over or replaced *(page 31)*. If the bottoms of the drawer

sides have worn down, they can be rebuilt with new wood *(page 32)*.

Replace worn metal guides with the same type. Wooden drawer guides can be replaced *(page 32)*, but a simpler remedy is to install drawer-glide buttons on the guides; these vinyl-coated or metal disks, similar to large thumbtacks, lift the drawer enough to let it slide smoothly.

If all the joints are loose, take apart the drawer and reglue the joints *(pages 30-31)*. Do not disassemble a drawer with a single loose joint; instead inject glue into it and clamp it.

Doors: To tighten a loose hinge, remove the screws, squirt a little

wood glue into the holes, and drive in the screws; or, plug the holes with dowels and drill new screw holes.

To disguise a warp in a door with surface-mounted hinges, you may be able to realign it by moving the hinges slightly *(page 33)*. A binding door can be righted by creating or deepening a hinge mortise *(page 34)*. As a last resort, plane the edges of the door *(page 34)*.

Casters: A cabinet that is not level is susceptible to joint failure. Replace broken or bent casters, or mount new casters that complement the design of the cabinet *(pages 34-35)*.

 TOOLS

Rubber mallet
Wood chisel
Screwdriver
Pipe or bar clamps
C-clamps
Tape measure

Handsaw
Nippers
Pry bar
Block plane
Rabbet plane
Electric drill
Pliers
Hammer

 **MATERIALS**

Wood glue
Hardwood stock
Replacement
 plywood

Replacment nails
 and screws
Paraffin
Dowels
Casters

 **SAFETY TIPS**

Protect your eyes with goggles when operating a power tool.

Anatomy of a cabinet frame.

In a typical cabinet, the base and sides fit together with rabbet joints. Two cleats set in the rabbet at the top of the sides anchor screws driven up into the top. The back—thin plywood or hardboard—is nailed into rabbets in the cabinet sides. The leg-and-apron assembly has mortise-and-tenon joints, much like those of a table *(page 21)*.

The front of most cabinets is enclosed by drawers or doors. Drawers rest on dust-panel frames held in dadoes in the cabinet sides; the dust panels are thin sheets of plywood set in a groove on the inside edges of their frames. Doors are hinged on a frame fastened to the front edges of the cabinet.

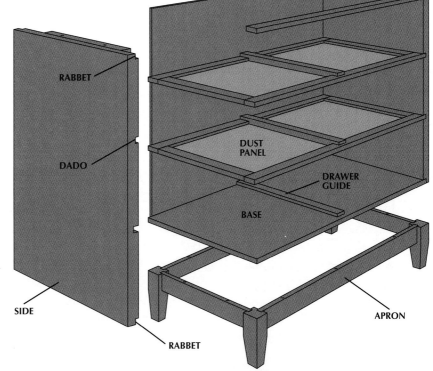

REGLUING A DRAWER

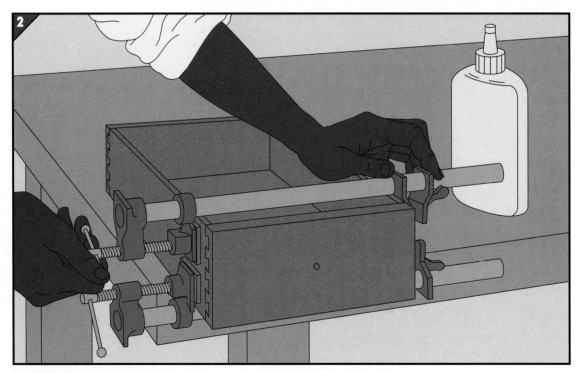

1. Knocking the drawer apart.

◆ A loose dovetail joint can often be separated by striking the side of the drawer with your hand. If this doesn't work, place a wood block along the drawer side in the loose corner and strike the block sharply with a mallet or hammer *(right)*, then separate the other corners. Disengage loose double-dado joints *(inset)* in the same way.

◆ With a chisel, scrape dirt and glue from the joint.

◆ Remove the drawer handle to facilitate clamping in Step 2.

DOUBLE-DADO JOINT

DOVETAIL JOINT

2. Gluing the joints.

◆ Apply wood glue to all the mating surfaces of the drawer and reassemble it.

◆ Protecting the drawer with wood pads, install pipe or bar clamps across the top and bottom of the drawer $\frac{1}{2}$ inch behind the dovetails at the front of the drawer *(above)*.

◆ Rest the drawer on its front and install clamps in the same way at the back of the drawer.

◆ Measure the two diagonals to ensure the drawer is square. If the measurements are not equal, shift the clamps as necessary.

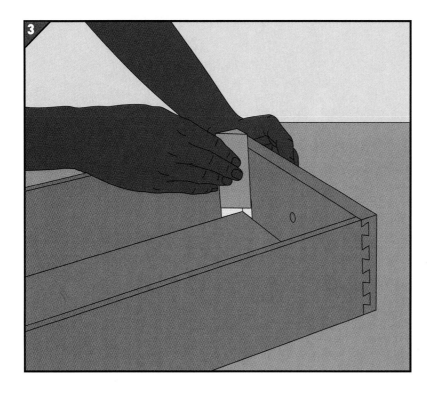

3. Adding glue blocks.
◆ Cut four triangular hardwood blocks equal in length to the width of the drawer sides.
◆ Spread an even coat of wood glue on two adjoining faces of a block and press it into one corner of the drawer, being careful not to get any glue on the drawer bottom.
◆ Rub the block up and down about $\frac{1}{2}$ inch until the glue begins to resist movement, then set the block in place.
◆ Glue a block in the remaining corners the same way.

REMEDIES FOR DRAWERS THAT STICK

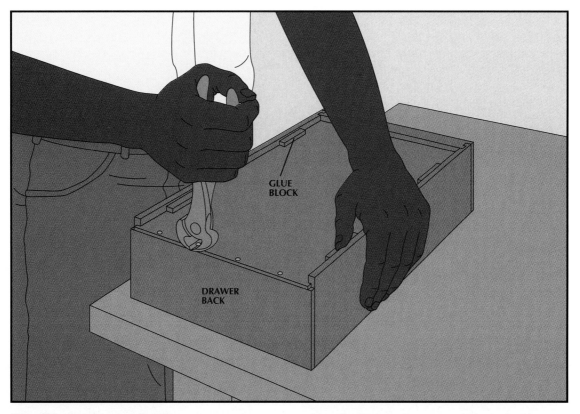

GLUE BLOCK

DRAWER BACK

Repairing a drawer bottom.
◆ Turn the drawer over. With nippers, pull out the nails securing the bottom to the back *(above)*.
◆ Remove any glue blocks from the bottom with a small pry bar or chisel.
◆ Slide the bottom out of its dadoes in the sides.

Where the bottom fits into a dado in the drawer back, disassemble the drawer *(opposite, Step 1)*.
◆ If the bottom is merely warped, turn it over. When it is split, replace it with a piece of plywood of the same dimensions.
◆ Reassemble the drawer.

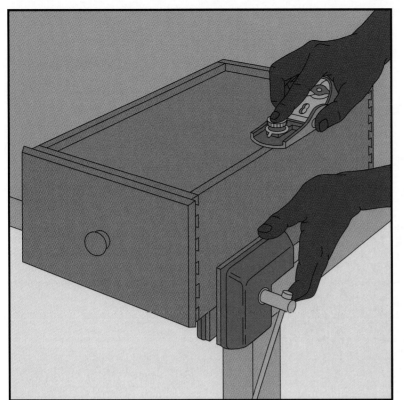

Rebuilding drawer sides.

◆ Secure the drawer—or the side piece if the drawer is disassembled—upside down in a woodworking vise.

◆ With a block plane, shave the edge of each side just enough to straighten and flatten it *(left)*—you will probably need to remove more wood at the back than the front. Use a chisel to remove wood the plane cannot reach.

◆ Cut two strips of hardwood to the size of the wood you removed.

◆ Glue the strips to the planed edges, place a long board on each strip, and secure the assemblies with large C-clamps until the glue has dried.

◆ Test-fit the drawer and, if necessary, plane or sand the new strips.

◆ Rub paraffin or a bar of soap along the bottom edges of the drawer sides to help them slide more easily.

Replacing wooden guides.

Many wooden drawers glide with the help of cleats and guides or grooves. Commonly, two cleats on the drawer bottom form a channel that slides on a guide in the center of the cabinet dust-panel frame, with the bottom edges of the drawer sides sliding on the sides of the frame *(right)*. Alternatively, cleats attached to the drawer sides slide in grooves in the cabinet sides *(inset, left)*; or the drawer sides have the grooves and the cleats are attached to the cabinet *(inset, right)*.

To replace a cleat, first trace its outline, then pry it free. Cut a hardwood duplicate and fasten it in the same position; use glue to attach it to a drawer, and both glue and screws to secure it to a cabinet.

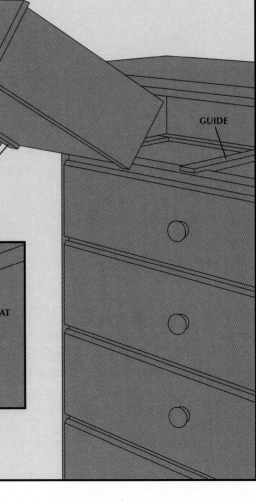

GUIDE

CLEATS

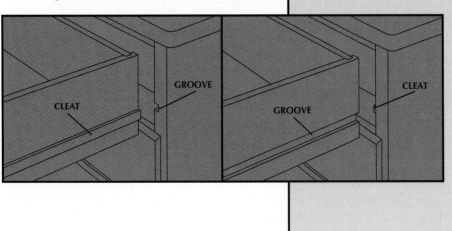

GROOVE

CLEAT

CLEAT

GROOVE

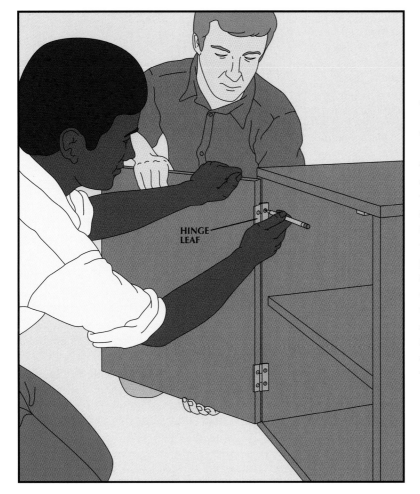

Adjusting a door.

If one corner on the unhinged side of a cabinet door protrudes when the door is closed, the door is probably warped.

◆ For a flush-mounted door, measure the displacement at the protruding corner.

◆ Unscrew the hinge leaves from the cabinet, remove the door, and plug the screw holes with wood glue and dowels.

◆ With a helper holding the door in position, move the hinge directly opposite the protruding corner inward on the cabinet frame by a distance equal to one-half the measured displacement. Mark the new screw holes *(left)*, then move the other hinge outward by an equal amount and mark its holes.

◆ Drill pilot holes and reattach the hinge leaves.

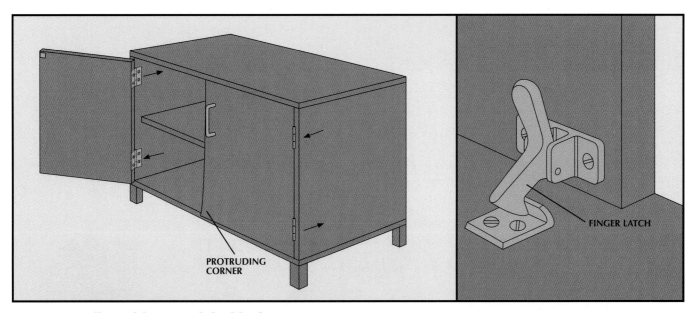

Dealing with warped double doors.

If both doors that meet at the middle of a cabinet are warped, adjust each one individually as explained above. If only one door is warped, measure the displacement of the protruding corner. Use the technique above, and adjust each hinge on the warped door by one-quarter of the measurement; repeat the procedure on the straight door, but shift the hinges in the opposite directions *(above, left)*.

Alternatively, install a finger latch in the cabinet *(above, right)* to hold the warped corner straight.

Freeing a binding edge.

On doors that stick just below the top corner or along the bottom edge, or double doors that rub together at the top, the top hinge is the problem. If the door binds along the top edge, the bottom hinge is at fault.

◆ If the hinge screws are loose, remove them, squirt wood glue in their holes, and let it dry. When the screws are not loose, unscrew the hinge leaves from the cabinet and remove the door. With a mallet and chisel, deepen the mortise of the faulty hinge by $\frac{1}{16}$ inch *(right)*; if there is no mortise, cut a shallow one.

◆ Screw the hinge back in place and check the swing of the door. If the edge still binds, plane it *(below)*.

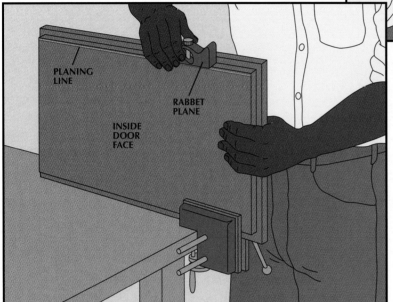

Planing a door.

◆ With the door closed, run a piece of paper around its edges to locate the binding spots; then mark them.

◆ Unscrew the hinges from the cabinet and remove the door.

◆ Draw a line on the door's inside face $\frac{1}{8}$ inch from the binding spot.

◆ Secure the door in a woodworking vise so the line is horizontal. On a lipped door, cut the inside lip down to the marked line with a rabbet plane *(left)*. On a flush door, bevel the edge down to the line with a block plane, removing as little wood as possible from the edge at the outside face of the door.

CHOOSING CASTERS

Two basic designs.

The two most common types of casters differ primarily in the way they are attached to furniture. Plate-mounted casters *(near right)*, which seldom require attention, are screwed directly to the underside of the piece; however, they cannot be mounted on small areas, such as a narrow leg. Here, stem casters are necessary *(far right)*. The shaft of a stem caster slips into a matching sleeve that fits into a hole in the end of the leg. The shaft can work loose in the sleeve or the sleeve loose in its hole. Replace a faulty stem caster with a plate-mounted model whenever possible; otherwise, attach another stem caster *(opposite)*.

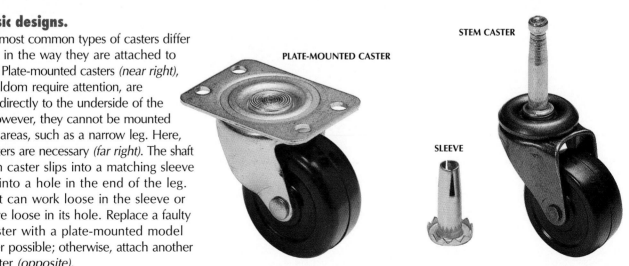

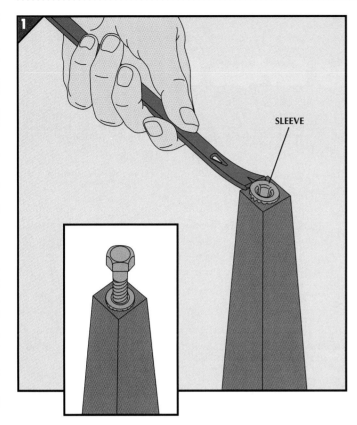

SLEEVE

1. Preparing the leg for a new caster.

◆ Pull the caster out of its sleeve.

◆ Work the clawed end of a small pry bar under the serrated flange of the sleeve and pry it out of its hole *(left)*. If the sleeve is stuck, tap a threaded bolt of about the same diameter into the sleeve opening just until it is wedged tight *(inset)*. Gripping the bolt with pliers, work the sleeve loose and out of its socket.

◆ Select a drill bit the same diameter as the sleeve on the next larger size of stem caster. Mark the length of the new sleeve on the bit with masking tape. Center the drill bit on the end of the leg and drill a hole for the sleeve, stopping when the tape contacts the surface.

If the leg is too small to allow a larger hole, plug the original hole by gluing in a dowel, then drill a hole for a stem caster one size smaller than the old one.

2. Installing a new caster.

◆ With a hammer and a wood block, tap the sleeve into its hole until the serrated flange bites into the wood *(near right)*.

◆ Push the caster's shaft into the sleeve; if necessary, tap lightly on a wood block held against the collar next to the wheel *(far right)*.

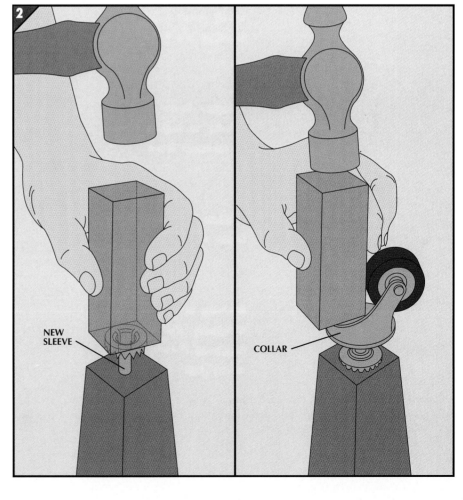

NEW SLEEVE

COLLAR

Mending Breaks and Surface Damage

Furniture hobbled by broken parts or defaced by dents and gouges can usually be restored. The trick is to effect inconspicuous repairs that leave the furniture as strong as new. This chapter presents techniques for patching solid-wood and veneer surfaces, splicing broken parts, closing cracks in table tops, and renewing woven chair seats.

Fixing a blister in veneer →

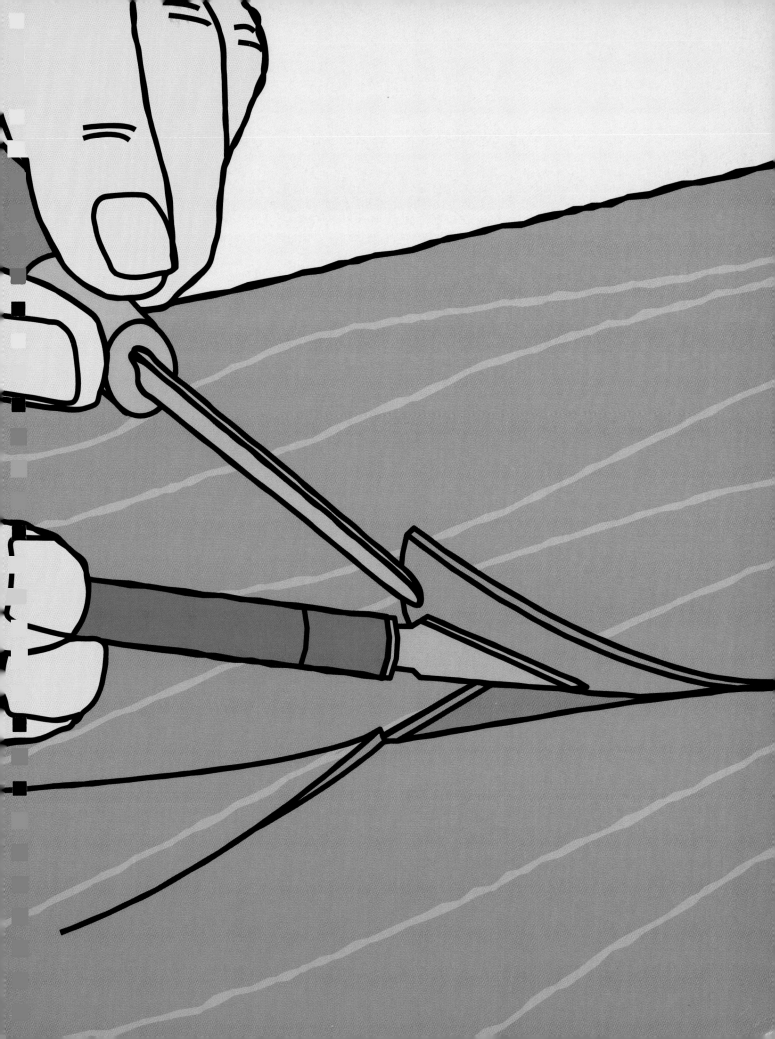

Remedies for Bruised and Bent Wood

Solid-wood furniture is vulnerable to scratching, gouging, and warping. Minor injuries on a very old piece are often left alone—on an antique, slight imperfections can lend character. Repair major damage using a method appropriate for the problem, and for the age and value of the piece.

Spot Repairs: A scratch in the finish can be filled with a wax stick *(page 69)*. Before treating dents or chipped edges, thoroughly clean the affected area and remove the finish with very fine sandpaper. A small dent can be raised with water or steam *(below and opposite)*. More extensive damage can be repaired with wood putty, which dries rapidly, comes in tints to match many woods, and can usually be stained. But before applying putty, test it with any stain you plan to use. If wood has broken off—chipped edges and corners are common—reshape the area with a mold *(opposite)*.

Warping: Wood sometimes warps when one side of a board is finished and the other is not, or when the board is not securely fastened to its understructure. Moisture enters the unfinished side and causes the wood to curl. Warps can sometimes be corrected with steam. Disassemble the piece, remove the finish, then set the warped part concave side up on a flat surface. Place a moist cloth on top, and pass an iron over the cloth. Or, on a sunny day, put the part, concave side down, on a damp lawn and place weights on top. Within a day or two, the warp should be gone. In either case, immediately refasten the part to its support when the warp relaxes, and refinish it when the wood is dry. If this does not eliminate the warp, try the method shown on page 40.

TOOLS

Artist's brush	Putty knife
Iron	Sanding block
Edge clamps	Circular saw
C-clamps	Electric drill
	Counterbore bit
	Screwdriver

MATERIALS

Paraffin	Felt
Wood putty	Finishing materials
1 x 2 for saw guide	Stock and nails
Sandpaper	for corner mold
(very fine grade)	Hardwood
	Wood screws
	(No. 8)

SAFETY TIPS

Protect your eyes with goggles when operating a power tool.

LIFTING A DENT

Raising the wood fibers.
◆ Apply water to the dent with an artist's brush or a finger tip, taking care not to wet the surrounding area *(right)*.
◆ Wait 30 minutes, and unless the crushed wood fibers are raised slightly above the level of the surrounding surface, brush on more water and wait again.
◆ If the fibers still have not risen, brush water on again, place a damp cloth over the dent, and hold an iron set at low heat against the cloth for 15 seconds. Repeat the steaming process, if necessary. If this is not effective, prick the surface with a pin and repeat the process to channel steam into the fibers.
◆ Allow the wood to dry thoroughly, then sand the area and finish it *(pages 73-81)*.

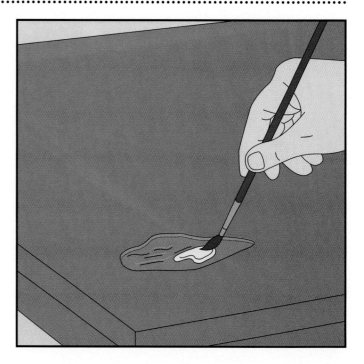

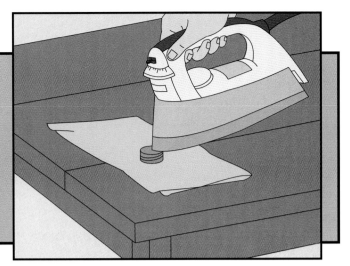

Focusing the Heat

For tiny dents or nicks close to glue joints, you can raise the crushed fibers with steam, but you must confine the steaming process to a very small area to avoid loosening the joint. Cover the affected area with a folded wet cloth, then place a bottle cap open-side down on the cloth over the dent, and hold the iron against the cap.

REBUILDING EDGES AND CORNERS

Filling in chipped edges.

◆ Rub paraffin or a wax crayon on one face of a board cut long enough to span the damaged area.
◆ Protecting the furniture with wood pads, clamp the waxed face of the board against the edge of the piece using edge clamps or C-clamps with wedges.
◆ With a putty knife, force wood putty into the nick *(right)*. If it is deeper or longer than $\frac{1}{4}$ inch, build up the putty in layers, giving each coat time to dry. Overfill the depression slightly.
◆ When the putty is dry, remove the board and, with very fine sandpaper, smooth the surface.
◆ Stain the patch *(pages 76-77)* and, if necessary, paint on grain *(page 69)*. Finish the patch *(pages 78-81)*.

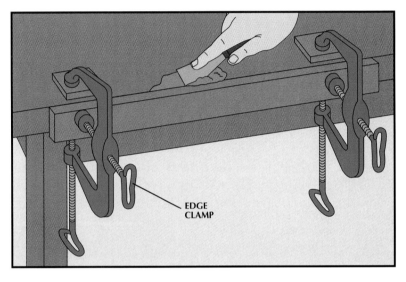

EDGE CLAMP

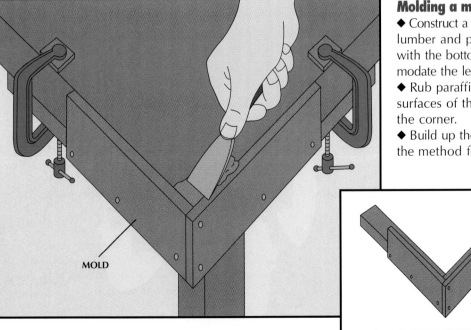

MOLD

Molding a missing corner.

◆ Construct a mold to fit the corner, using smooth lumber and plywood *(inset)*. If a leg interferes with the bottom piece, adapt the mold to accommodate the leg.
◆ Rub paraffin or a wax crayon on the inside surfaces of the mold and clamp the mold to the corner.
◆ Build up the corner with wood putty, following the method for a chipped edge *(left)*.

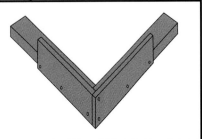

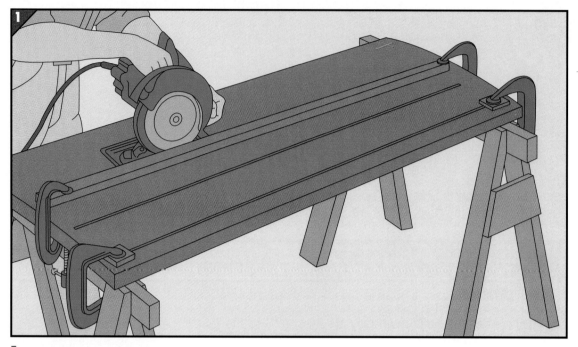

1. Kerfing the underside.

◆ With wood pads protecting the piece, clamp it bottom up to a work surface.
◆ Set the depth of a circular saw blade to half the thickness of the wood.
◆ To guide the saw, clamp a 1-by-2 along one edge of the piece parallel with the grain direction.

◆ Cut a kerf into the surface, starting and stopping 1 inch short of the ends. Working toward the opposite edge, make three more evenly spaced kerfs in the piece *(above)*.
◆ If the warp persists, cut additional kerfs, keeping them evenly spaced and at least 2 inches apart. If the piece still isn't flat, attach battens *(Step 2)*.

2. Attaching battens.

◆ Cut two hardwood battens $\frac{3}{4}$ inch thick, $1\frac{1}{2}$ inches wide, and almost as long as the width of the piece. Bevel the ends of the battens so they won't show from the top.
◆ Clamp the battens to the underside of the piece, 8 to 10 inches from each end, or where they will not interfere with the legs or frame when the piece is reassembled.
◆ Positioning the bit between kerfs, drill countersunk pilot holes for No. 8 wood screws into the battens at 6-inch intervals, staggered in a W pattern. Stop each hole $\frac{1}{4}$ inch from the top surface of the table top.
◆ Drive the first screw where the batten touches the high point of the warp *(right)*. Tighten the clamps on the batten slightly and drive the remaining screws, working toward the low points of the warp and tightening the clamps after each screw is driven.

Mending Veneer

The surface of a fine piece of furniture is likely to be veneer—a thin layer of decorative wood glued over a core of less attractive wood or plywood. Damage to veneer, if limited to small areas, can often be repaired with scarcely a trace.

Surface Blemishes: The glue used to apply old veneers may fail in places, resulting in blisters. To repair a blister, try placing a cloth on it and warming the surface with an iron set at medium heat to soften the glue. Then weight the area with heavy books for several hours to press the veneer back into place. If the blister remains, cut through it and apply fresh glue *(pages 42-43)*. Chipped or burned veneer can be patched by cutting out the damage and fitting a new piece *(pages 43-44)*. The veneer on some older furniture may be so thick that you will have to glue down more than one layer to bring the patch to the level of the surface.

Plastic Laminates: Used on less expensive furniture, these surface treatments are usually attached with contact cement. Repair a lifted edge by scraping the old cement from both surfaces, spreading fresh cement on them, and pressing the laminate back in place after waiting the amount of time specified on the product label—no clamping is required. Chipped laminate can be repaired the same way if the chip is intact. If not, fill the damaged area with wood putty *(page 39)*.

 TOOLS

Craft knife
Metal straightedge
Palette knife
Putty knife
Wallpaper
  seam roller
Wood chisel
Mallet

 **MATERIALS**

Wood glue
Wax paper
Cardboard
Veneer for patch
Wood putty
Felt
Sandpaper
  (very fine grade)
Finishing materials

SELECTING VENEER

Veneers are cut from a wide variety of woods; varied patterns are achieved by slicing the veneer from different parts of the tree *(photographs)*. When buying veneer for patching—craft stores usually have a large selection—choose one that matches the grain of the original and is slightly lighter in color. Buy a piece a little thicker than the original veneer and large enough to allow some leeway in choosing an area from which to cut the patch.

MAHOGANY CROTCH

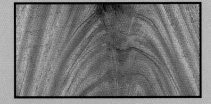

BIRD'S-EYE MAPLE

ELM BURL

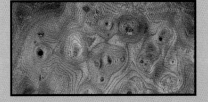

STRIPED ROSEWOOD

WALNUT BUTT

FLAT-CUT BEECH

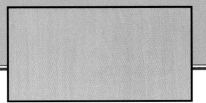

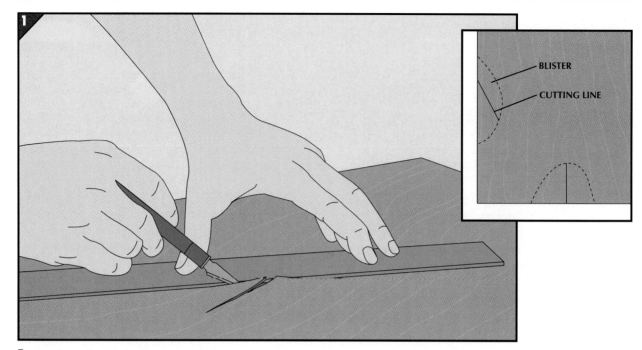

1. Cutting through the veneer.
◆ If the blister is in the middle of the surface, cut through it at a diagonal to the grain with a craft knife guided by a metal straightedge.
◆ Make a second diagonal cut through the blister that intersects the first, creating four flaps *(above)*.
◆ Press the veneer down into place; if necessary, shave slivers of veneer from the edges of the flaps until they lie flat.

For a blister at an edge, lift it and scrape out old glue *(Step 2)* without cutting through the veneer. If this is impossible, cut through the veneer—parallel to the grain if the edge is perpendicular to the grain; diagonally if the edge is parallel to the grain *(inset)*.

2. Applying fresh glue.
◆ Gently raise one flap of the blister with a small palette knife or putty knife and scrape old glue from the veneer and the underlying surface with a craft knife *(right)*. If the veneer does not bend up easily, dampen it with a few drops of warm water. Clean each flap, occasionally vacuuming away particles of old glue.
◆ If the veneer is damp, let it dry. Then, with a small putty knife or artist's brush, apply a thin coat of wood glue to the underlying surface.
◆ Press the veneer into place and wipe away any extruded glue.

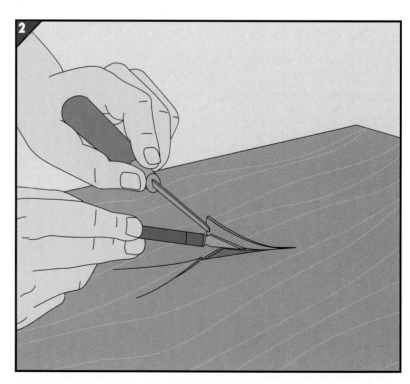

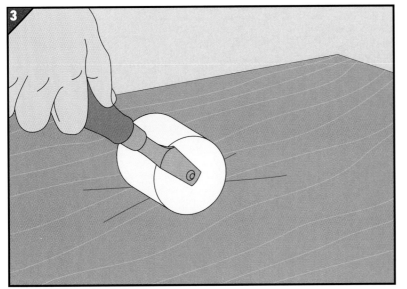

3. Setting the glue.

◆ With a wallpaper-seam roller, flatten the repair, pressing lightly at first, then gradually increasing the pressure *(left)*.

◆ Wipe away any extruded glue and place a piece of wax paper on the repair. Set a wood block larger than the repair on the paper and weight it down until the glue is dry.

◆ Remove the weights and paper, and refinish the area *(pages 73-81)*.

GRAFTING IN A PATCH

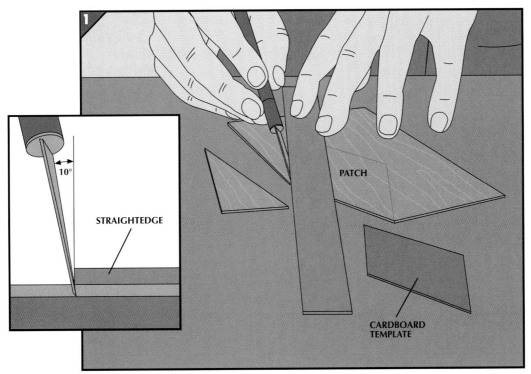

10°

STRAIGHTEDGE

PATCH

CARDBOARD TEMPLATE

1. Preparing the patch.

◆ From stiff cardboard, cut a template slightly larger than the damaged area, cutting a diamond shape if the damage is near the middle of the surface, or a V shape for damage at an edge.

◆ Set the template on the replacement veneer, orienting it so the grain of the patch will be parallel to the grain of the surface being repaired, and the pattern of the patch and surface will be a close match.

◆ Lightly score the outline of the template on the veneer with a sharp craft knife.

◆ Align a metal straightedge with one of the scored lines on the patch and run a craft knife tilted outward at a 10-degree angle along the edge *(inset)*; angling the knife will make the bottom of the patch smaller than the top, improving its fit. Make as many cuts as needed to slice through the veneer, then cut through the remaining scored lines in the same way *(above)*.

2. Cutting away the damage.

◆ Place the patch over the damaged area, aligning its grain with the surface grain, and score its outline with the craft knife.

◆ Remove the patch and, with the craft knife tilted against the straightedge as in Step 1, cut through the veneer at the scored lines.

◆ Starting at the center of the outline and working outward, remove the damaged veneer with a chisel held beveled side down *(right)*. If necessary, tap the chisel lightly with a mallet.

◆ Scrape any glue or dirt from the underlying wood with the chisel, occasionally cleaning away debris with a vacuum cleaner.

◆ If the surface under the veneer is damaged, level it with wood putty and let the putty dry.

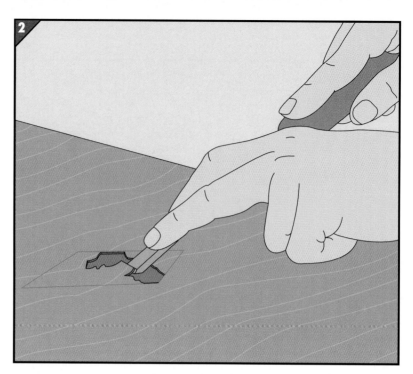

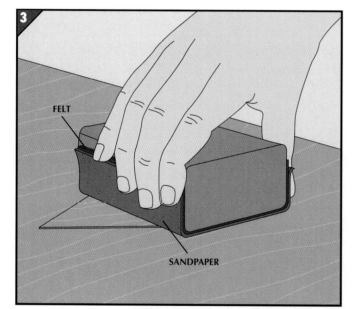

FELT

SANDPAPER

3. Fitting the patch in place.

◆ With a small putty knife or artist's brush, spread a thin layer of wood glue in the opening for the patch. Press the patch into place and wipe away any extruded glue.

◆ Roll and weight the patch *(page 43, Step 3)*. If the veneer sits lower than the surface, cut and glue a second layer.

◆ Smooth the patch with very fine sandpaper wrapped over a felt-covered block cut slightly larger than the patch, and with its edges rounded. Sand in the direction of the grain, using only light pressure, until the patch is flush with the surrounding surface *(left)*.

◆ Refinish the repair *(pages 73-81)*.

A VENEER PUNCH FOR A QUICK REPAIR

You can speed the process of repairing a small flaw by using a veneer punch. Protecting the surface with a cloth, first heat the area with an iron set at medium heat. Then, position the punch over the damage and strike it sharply with a hammer, scoring a circle around the blemish. Pull out the piece of veneer or remove it with a narrow chisel. Use the punch to cut a matching patch from a replacement piece.

Breaks in a piece of furniture create, in effect, joints where none were intended. Repairing such breaks must leave the part as strong as it was originally, while at the same time being as unobtrusive as possible. Depending on the type of break *(below)*, glue alone may do the job, or it may require the support of dowels or bracing blocks.

Repairs with Dowels: If a part is broken cleanly in two, a dowel can often be hidden within the piece *(pages 46-47).* But for a break at an extreme angle, or one located at a curve, it's best to insert one or two dowels from the outside, which will leave the ends of the dowels visible *(pages 48-49).*

In either case, use a dowel with a diameter about one-half the thickness of the part being mended and at least twice as long as that thickness. You can purchase precut dowels, or cut them to length from a dowel rod; the fluted type lets glue spread more evenly.

Adding Braces: Rectangular bracing blocks reinforce repairs in flat parts, such as chair-back splats and seat rails. In hidden areas, the brace can simply be fastened across the break *(page 49).* However, if the brace will be visible, cut it from wood matching the part and recess it in a mortise cut across the break.

Clamping: Install clamps on a repair so their force is applied perpendicular to the line of the break. Depending on the location and orientation of the damage, some ingenuity may be needed in the choice and placement of clamps.

 TOOLS

C-clamps	Rubber mallet
Pipe or	Handsaw
bar clamps	Upholstery
Electric drill	tools
Dowel jig	Screwdriver
Utility knife	Backsaw

 **MATERIALS**

Dowels	Wood screws
Wood glue	($\frac{3}{4}$" No. 6)
Hardwood stock	

 SAFETY TIPS

Put on goggles when using an electric drill.

Three types of break.

Wood that breaks jaggedly *(above, left)* provides two large, irregular surfaces that will make for an effective glue bond. Additional reinforcement is often unnecessary.

If the break is clean *(above, center)*, the surface area is too small and uniform for glue to bond.

In order to last, a repair will have to be strengthened with a brace or a dowel *(pages 46-47 and page 49).*

A break along a grain line *(above, right)* produces long, angled surfaces, but ones along a natural weak point. This kind of break needs to be reinforced with a dowel or brace *(pages 48-49).*

A HIDDEN DOWEL

1. Drilling holes for the dowel.

◆ For a clean break *(page 45)*, set the furniture broken end up; clamp it to a work surface if it is unsteady.

◆ Fit an electric drill with a bit of the same diameter as the dowel you'll be using to mend the break. Center the bit over the broken end of the furniture—using a dowel jig if the break is clean enough *(right)*, or center by eye if the break is irregular—and drill a hole to the depth of the thickness of the broken piece.

◆ Clamp the piece that broke off in a vise, protecting it with cloth padding, and make an identical hole in the broken end.

◆ Clean the debris out of the holes.

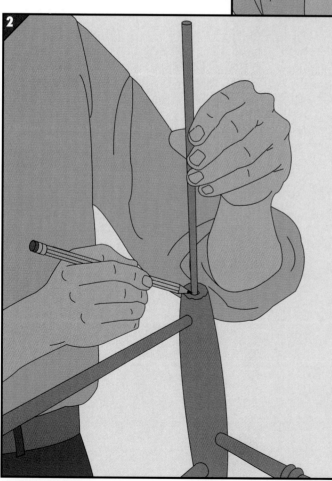

DOWEL JIG

2. Making the dowel peg.

◆ Insert a pencil or a thin dowel into each hole and mark the depth on it *(left)*.

◆ Cut the repair dowel $\frac{1}{4}$ inch shorter than the combined depths of the holes.

◆ With a utility knife, bevel the ends of the dowel slightly. If it isn't the fluted type, cut at least four grooves along its sides *(inset)*, or groove the dowel by drawing it through the teeth of pliers.

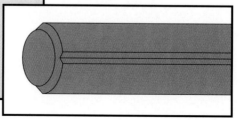

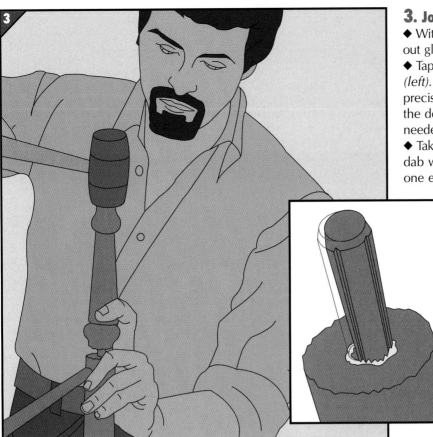

3. Joining the pieces.

◆ With a mallet, tap the dowel—without glue—into the hole in the furniture.

◆ Tap the loose piece onto the dowel *(left)*. If the broken ends don't align precisely, pare down the thickness of the dowel with a utility knife *(inset)* as needed to allow the pieces to line up.

◆ Take the dowel out of the hole and dab wood glue in one hole and on one end of the dowel, then tap the glued end of the dowel into the hole as far as it will go.

◆ Apply glue to the other hole, the other end of the dowel, and the broken surfaces, then tap the pieces together. Wipe off extruded glue.

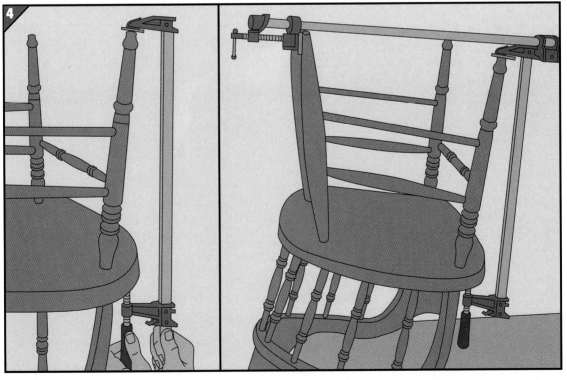

4. Clamping the repair.

Protecting the furniture with wood pads, install a pipe or bar clamp from one end of the broken part to the other so the bar or pipe is as perpendicular to the break as possible. If the clamp pulls the pieces out of alignment *(above, left)*, straighten them by installing a second clamp between one jaw of the first clamp and a furniture part opposite it *(above, right)*.

1. Drilling the dowel hole.

◆ Apply wood glue to the broken ends and squeeze them together with two C-clamps pressing two strips of wood against the sides of the piece.

◆ Fit an electric drill with a bit of the same diameter as the dowel you will use. At the least inconspicuous spot, drill a hole into the piece on one side of the break at a right angle to it; continue drilling partway into the other side of the break *(right)*.

◆ Vacuum wood chips and dust out of the hole.

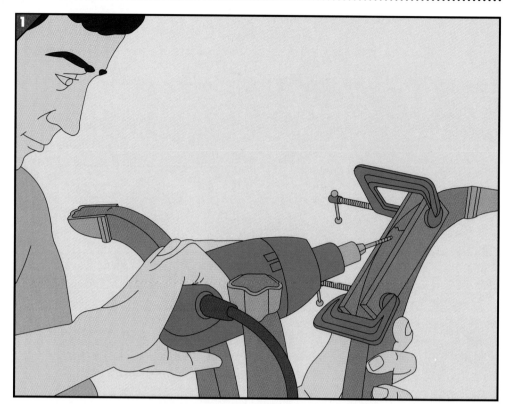

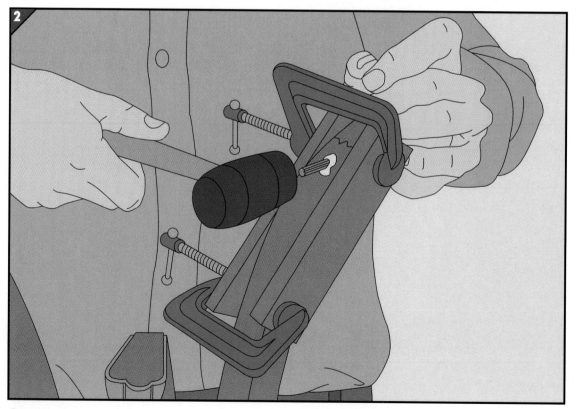

2. Inserting a dowel.

◆ Insert a pencil or thin dowel into the hole and mark its depth.

◆ Cut a dowel slightly longer than the measured depth, bevel one end, and groove it with a utility knife or pliers *(page 46, Step 2)*.

◆ Dab glue in the hole and on the dowel, and tap the dowel into the hole with a mallet *(above)*.

◆ Remove the clamps and wood supports, and wipe off extruded glue.

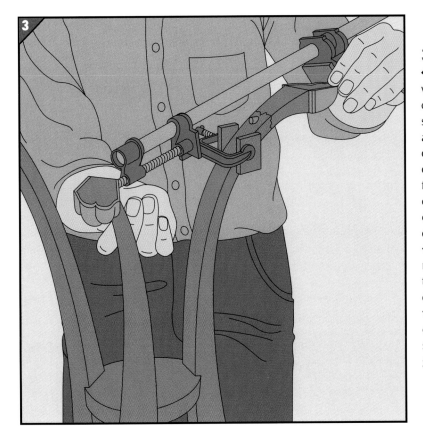

3. Clamping the splice.

◆ Protecting the furniture with wood pads, attach a C-clamp to the piece on one side of the break to provide a bearing surface for a pipe or bar clamp. Install this second clamp across the break from the C-clamp to the end of the broken part so the clamping pressure is perpendicular to the break *(left)*.

◆ Once the glue is dry, remove the clamps and trim the protruding end of the dowel flush with the surface with a backsaw or a flush-cutting saw; if necessary, sand it smooth with medium-grade sandpaper.

A CONCEALED BRACE

Fastening the brace.

◆ Expose as much as possible of the broken part; if the break is covered by upholstery, remove tacks or staples *(page 93, Step 1)* and carefully fold back the fabric for several inches on each side of the break.

◆ Spread wood glue on the broken ends and, protecting the piece with wood pads, clamp them together with a pipe or bar clamp running between the ends of the piece.

◆ Cut a rectangular brace of $\frac{1}{4}$-inch-thick hardwood as wide as the length of the break, and long enough to be fastened to solid wood on each side of the break.

◆ On the inconspicuous side of the broken part, position the brace over the break and drill a pilot hole at each corner for $\frac{3}{4}$-inch No. 6 wood screws.

◆ Spread wood glue on the brace and screw it in place.

◆ When the glue is dry, remove the clamp. Retack fabric if necessary.

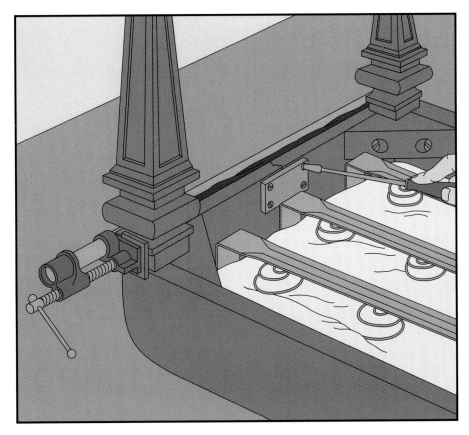

Over time, the individual boards of a table top may shrink and draw apart, producing cracks where they were glued together.

Closing a Narrow Crack: First, clean the edges of the crack with a thin blade and force glue into it with a glue injector *(page 11)*. Clamp the crack shut so the clamping pressure is perpendicular to the break; on a round or oval top, a pair of clamp cauls—boards that fit the curve—are helpful *(opposite)*.

Sawing Out a Straight Crack: For a crack that cannot be closed easily by clamping, remove the top from the leg assembly, then draw a line along the crack from one edge of the top to the other. Cut along the line with a table saw or a circular saw guided by a strip of wood clamped parallel to the crack. The two parts of the top can then be glued back together.

Filling a Wide Crack: For a crack that is too wide to clamp closed or saw out, fill it with a spline *(below)*.

TOOLS

Circular saw
Rubber mallet
Pipe or bar clamps

Backsaw
Wood chisel
Saber saw
Glue injector

MATERIALS

Hardwood stock
1 x 6s

Sandpaper
(medium grade,
very fine grade)
Wood glue

SAFETY TIPS

Put on goggles when operating a power saw.

A SPLINE FOR A WIDE BREAK

Filling the crack.

◆ With a circular saw, cut a spline with the grain, from matching wood. Cut it slightly longer than the crack and wider than the table's thickness; sand the spline with medium-grade sandpaper so it fits the crack snugly.

◆ Apply wood glue to both sides of the spline and insert it into the crack—from the edge for a short crack, or from the top for a long one. Tap the spline in gently with a mallet *(right)*, letting excess spline protrude.

◆ If the top is rectangular, apply pipe or bar clamps perpendicular to the crack; for a round or oval top, make clamp cauls *(opposite)*.

◆ When the glue is dry, remove the clamps. With a backsaw or flush-cutting saw, cut the spline flush with the edge of the table top. Then, with a chisel held bevel side down, pare the spline flush with the top face *(inset)*. Smooth the repair with very fine sandpaper and refinish the surface *(pages 76-81)*.

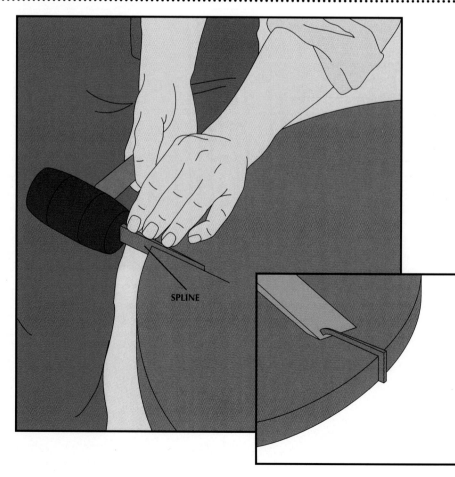

SPLINE

1. Making clamp cauls.
◆ Remove the top from the leg assembly and set it upside down on a pair of 1-by-6s. Position the boards parallel to each other and to the crack in the top so their outer edges are at least 2 inches beyond the circumference of the top.
◆ Trace the outline of the top on the boards *(left)*.
◆ Cut along the lines with a saber saw.

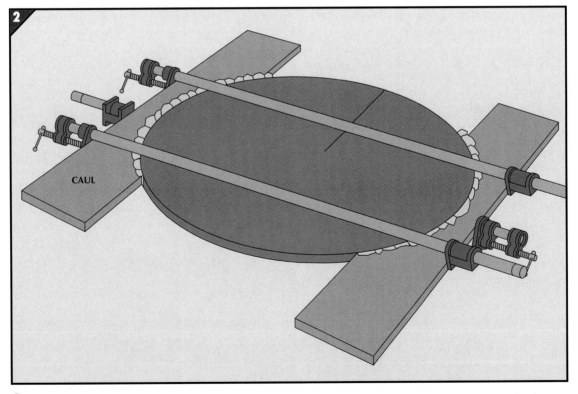

CAUL

2. Clamping the top.
◆ Pad the edge of the top with cloth, felt, or rubber cut from an old inner tube, and position the cauls against it opposite each other.
◆ Apply wood glue inside the crack, using a glue injector if necessary *(page 11)*.

◆ Orient two pipe or bar clamps perpendicular to the crack and install them between the straight edges of the cauls. If you use more than two clamps, alternate their positions—across the underside and top surface *(above)*—to prevent the top from warping.

The techniques for making woven chair seats have been known and used for a very long time. The three most popular weaving materials today are rush, splint, and cane *(opposite)*. Each material is woven in a traditional pattern, and it is best to reweave a seat with the original type of fiber. If a chair has no seat, the construction of the seat frame can help you determine the fiber *(below)*.

Preparing for the Job: Remove all traces of the existing woven material, repair broken seat-frame parts, and refinish the chair, if necessary.

Each weaving material is prepared in a different manner. Soak splint—only five to six strands at a time—in a bucket of lukewarm water for 15 minutes before weaving. Coil it with its smooth side out—the side that doesn't splinter when the strand is bent between your fingers. Then, round the splint at both ends with scissors. For fiber rush, dip a 20-foot length in water for about 30 seconds. For cane, soak the strands in lukewarm water for 15 minutes; prewoven caning requires about an hour of soaking. Coil cane strands in a bucket, with the shiny side out. Lay prewoven cane flat in a bathtub.

Finishing the Seat: When the weaving is complete, remove stray hairs from splint and cane with tweezers or scissors. You can stain a splint-woven seat or let it darken with age. Cane will also darken naturally; for a high-gloss finish, apply a lacquer sealer, followed by clear lacquer. For a fiber-rush seat, brush on one or two coats of shellac, and repeat this application once a year to prolong the life of the fiber.

TOOLS

SPLINT
Tack hammer
Scissors
Spring clamps
Standard stapler
Pliers
Screwdriver

FIBER RUSH
Tack hammer
Scissors
Spring clamps
Drafting triangle
Rubber mallet
Spring clamps

PREWOVEN CANE
Scissors
Utility knife
Screwdriver
Shop knife
Rubber mallet
Hardwood wedges
Razor blade
Tweezers

HANDWOVEN CANE
Caning pegs
Scissors
Handsaw
Mallet
Sanding block

MATERIALS

SPLINT
Standard staples
Carpet tacks ($\frac{3}{16}$")

FIBER RUSH
Carpet tacks ($\frac{3}{16}$")
Cardboard

PREWOVEN CANE
Reed spline
Wood glue

HANDWOVEN CANE
Binder cane
Wood glue
Sandpaper
 (medium grade)

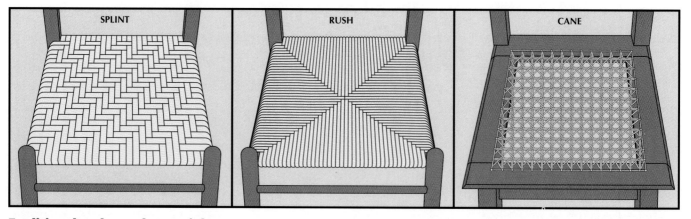

Traditional styles and materials.

The methods for weaving chair seats differ, depending on whether the material is splint, rush, or cane. Both splint and rush are wrapped around the outside of round or oval seat rails. For splint, strands called warp are wrapped around the side rails, then pieces called weavers are wrapped around the front and back rails, passing over and under groups of three strands of warp to create a herringbone pattern *(above, left)*. With rush, the fibers are wrapped in a continuous fashion around the four posts and rails to create a triangular pattern *(above, center)*. Cane is woven through holes drilled around the perimeter of the seat frame. Commonly, strands are laid side-to-side, front-to-back, and diagonally to create an open diamond pattern *(above, right)*. Prewoven cane fits into a groove around the seat and is held there with a flexible spline *(pages 57-59)*.

Splint, rush, cane strands, and prewoven cane are available from handicraft shops and mail-order suppliers specializing in basketry and caning materials.

Splint: Originally cut from the inner bark of hickory and ash trees, most splint—the so-called flat-reed type—is now derived from the core of the rattan vine. It is made in various widths—$\frac{3}{8}$ and $\frac{1}{2}$ inch are most common for chair seats—and is sold by the bundle. One bundle will generally cover an average-size seat. Though more expensive and harder to use, traditional ash splint is still available for restoring a chair with original materials. Fiber splint made of kraft paper is also available, but can be used only on chairs that will not be exposed to moisture.

Fiber Rush: This cordlike material is made from kraft paper, twisted by machine to resemble natural rush (cattail leaves). Widths range from   to $\frac{1}{4}$ inch. The most durable seating material, fiber rush comes in an array of earthy colors. It is sold by weight; about 2 pounds will cover an average-size chair seat.

Cane: Cut from the outer bark of the rattan plant, cane strands are sold in widths and thicknesses suited to the size and spacing of the holes in the seat frame. The most common sizes are fine, narrow-medium, and medium. Fine cane is for holes $\frac{3}{16}$ inch in diameter, spaced $\frac{1}{2}$ to $\frac{9}{16}$ inch from center to center; narrow-medium is for holes $\frac{1}{4}$ inch in diameter, $\frac{5}{8}$ inch center to center; and medium is for holes $\frac{1}{4}$ inch in diameter, $\frac{3}{4}$ inch center to center. Cane is sold in hanks of 350 to 1,000 feet, composed of individual 8- to 12-foot strands. A 350-foot hank covers an average seat.

Prewoven Cane: Also called cane webbing, this material consists of strands of natural cane loom-woven into various patterns. The traditional six-way pattern shown below is sized according to the distance from the center of one hole in the pattern to the center of the next; sizes range from $\frac{3}{8}$ to 1 inch. It is available in rolls 12 to 36 inches wide, from which suppliers will cut pieces to size, based on the dimensions of the chair seat. Buy a piece to bridge the widest part of the seat, measured from the outside edges of the groove, adding 1 inch for the material that will be fitted into the groove. A reed spline, which is driven into the groove to hold the cane in place, is sold by the foot in widths to match the groove.

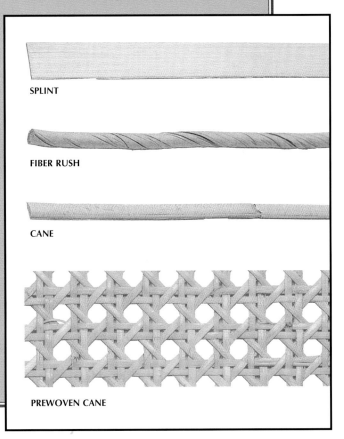

SPLINT

FIBER RUSH

CANE

PREWOVEN CANE

WORKING WITH SPLINT

1. Wrapping the warp.

◆ Prepare the splint as described on page 52.

◆ Position the rough side of one end of a strand of splint against the inside face of the back rail at one end. Secure the splint with a $\frac{3}{16}$-inch carpet tack.

◆ Keeping the smooth side of the splint exposed, pull the splint under the opposite side rail, up and over the rail, and across to and around the other side rail; do not pull it completely tight as you wrap.

◆ Continue wrapping the splint in the same way *(right)*. After the last complete pass you can make across the top of the seat, cut off the splint, leaving an end of 6 to 8 inches; spring-clamp the end to the nearest side rail. Splice a new strand to the first one with three standard staples, overlapping the strands by about 3 inches *(inset)*. Squeeze the staples shut with pliers.

◆ Keep wrapping, splicing as necessary, until the side rails are covered. Then clamp the final strand to a side rail; tack the loose end to the inside of the front rail and cut it off.

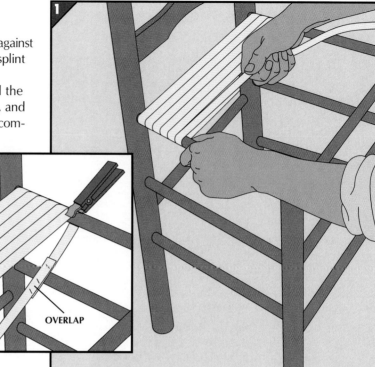

OVERLAP

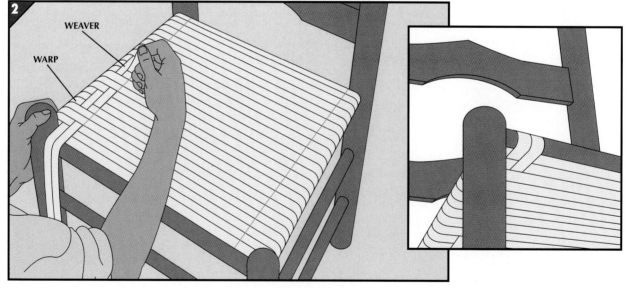

WEAVER

WARP

2. Squaring an angled seat.

Where the front rail is longer than the back one, you will need to fill a triangular area on each side with short rows when adding the front-to-back weavers:

◆ Measure the front and back rails, divide the difference in half, and mark this distance from each end of the front rail.

◆ Dampen the warp splints on the left third of the seat with a sponge.

◆ At the left front corner, draw a weaver over the first two strands of warp, then under and over strands in groups of three; keep the splint parallel with the pencil line. When the strand butts into the side rail, tuck it under a warp strand; at the front rail, trim it to a length equal to the length of the piece you wove into the top of the seat.

◆ Add another strand, first passing over three warp strands and then under and over groups of three *(above)*. To fill a larger triangular area, pass a weaver under one warp splint at the front rail. For the next two rows, at the front rail offset each weaver by one warp strand; after passing under three warp strands, start the pattern again by passing over one warp thread, and so on.

◆ Turn the chair upside down and weave the loose strands through the bottom layer of warp, maintaining the same pattern as on top *(inset)*. Tuck the ends into the space between the top and bottom warp.

3. Completing the pattern.

◆ Starting next to the completed triangle, weave a strand from the front rail to the back, continuing the pattern described in Step 2. Pull the excess through, leaving a loose end at the front rail equal to the length of the side rails. Weave this end into the underside of the chair.

◆ Carry the splint over the back rail, weave it back through the bottom layer of warp, then start a new row on top. Snug up each new row of splint and, when you come to the end of a strand, splice a new strand on the underside of the seat as you did in Step 1.

◆ When you have completed one-third of the seat, let the splint dry for 24 hours, then adjust the weavers sideways to fill any gaps that have opened up between them.

◆ For the middle third and the right third of the seat, wet the warp splints and repeat the weaving process. With a blunt screwdriver, lift tight warp splints enough to slide the weaver through *(right)*.

◆ When the last row before the pencil mark on the right is woven, cut the splint, leaving a loose end equal to the length of the side rails; weave this end into the bottom of the seat.

◆ Fill in the right-hand triangle *(Step 2)*.

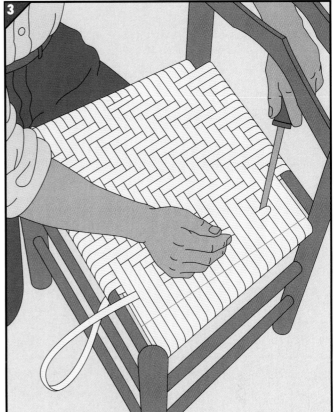

WRAPPING FIBER RUSH

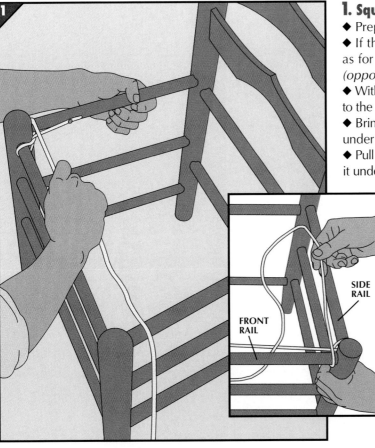

FRONT RAIL

SIDE RAIL

1. Squaring the seat.

◆ Prepare the rush as described on page 52.

◆ If the front rail is longer than the back one, measure it as for a splint seat and mark the front rail on each side *(opposite, Step 2)*.

◆ With $\frac{3}{16}$-inch carpet tacks, fasten one end of a length of rush to the inside face of the left rail, 3 inches from the front corner.

◆ Bring the cord under, then over the front rail; loop it back under itself, then under and over the left rail *(left)*.

◆ Pull the cord across to the opposite side of the seat, and loop it under and over the right rail; then carry it back under itself, and under and over the front rail *(inset)*. Tack it to the inside of the right rail, directly across from the tack on the left rail.

◆ Tack a second length of cord to the inside of the left rail, 1 inch behind the first, and wrap it in the same pattern. Continue until you have filled the triangular areas between the front corner posts and the pencil marks on the front rails. On each pass, pull the cord taut across the seat but relax pressure while wrapping the corners.

◆ With a drafting triangle, check that the intersecting cords are at right angles. If the cords are spread out, gently tap them into line with a rubber mallet and a small wood block; if they ride up on each other, flatten them with a mallet.

2. Completing a circuit.

◆ Tack one end of a length of rush to the left side rail, just beyond the previous cord. Wrap it around the two front corners *(Step 1)*, but instead of tacking it to the right rail, continue the pattern to the right back corner, then to the left back corner *(left and inset)*.

◆ Continue wrapping until the cord runs out. Then attach a new length of cord to the loose end with a square knot, positioning it so the knot is on the underside of the chair at a point that parallels the side rails.

◆ After about every six circuits, secure the cord to a rail with a spring clamp, and adjust the cords as you did at the end of Step 1.

3. Stuffing the seat.

◆ When only about 4 inches of each side rail is left exposed, cut four triangles of corrugated cardboard to fit into the pocket between the upper and lower layers of rush at both sides and at the front and back. Snip off the upper point of each triangle.

◆ Slide each triangle between the layers of rush *(right)*. If the front and back rails are lower than the side rails, insert additional layers of cardboard to fill the pockets.

◆ Continue weaving until the side rails are filled.

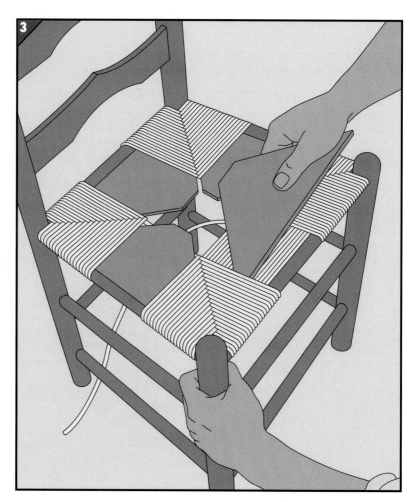

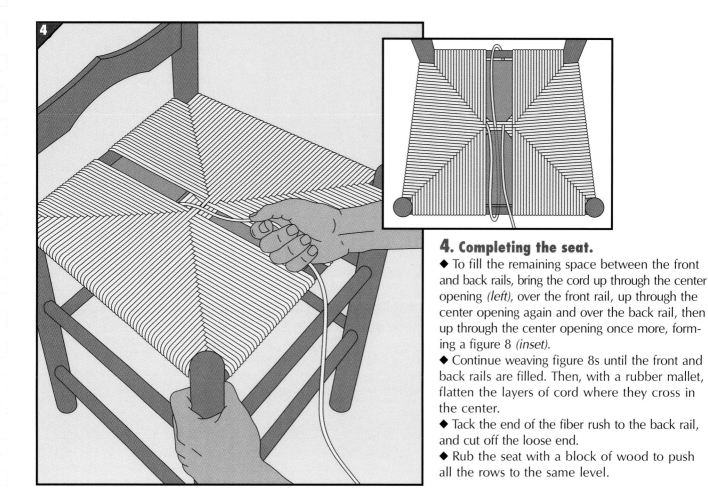

4. Completing the seat.

◆ To fill the remaining space between the front and back rails, bring the cord up through the center opening *(left)*, over the front rail, up through the center opening again and over the back rail, then up through the center opening once more, forming a figure 8 *(inset)*.

◆ Continue weaving figure 8s until the front and back rails are filled. Then, with a rubber mallet, flatten the layers of cord where they cross in the center.

◆ Tack the end of the fiber rush to the back rail, and cut off the loose end.

◆ Rub the seat with a block of wood to push all the rows to the same level.

REPLACING PREWOVEN CANE

1. Removing the old seat.

◆ Cut a large X through the damaged caning material with strong scissors.

◆ Run a utility knife along both edges of the groove in the seat frame to loosen the spline.

◆ Pry out the spline with a screwdriver *(right)* or a special tool called a spline chisel, which has a bent tip to facilitate this task *(photograph)*. If the spline does not come out easily, remove as much of it as possible, then squirt a mixture of equal amounts of vinegar and water into the groove. Let the spline soak for several hours before removing the rest of it.

◆ Pull the seat material out of the groove.

◆ Scrape old glue out of the groove with a shop knife.

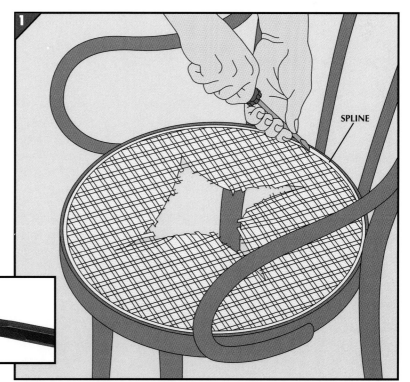

SPLINE

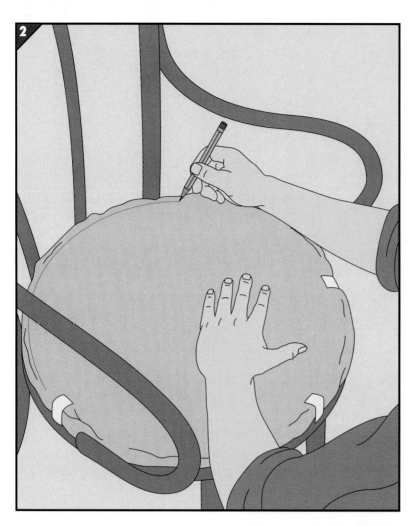

2. Cutting the pattern.
◆ Tape a piece of paper over the seat frame, run a pencil along the outside edge of the groove *(left)*, and cut along the marked line, creating a template of the seat.
◆ Tape the template onto a section of prewoven cane, positioning the pattern so one set of double strands runs straight down the middle from front to back, and another set will run parallel with the front rail—on a square seat—or in line with the front legs on a round seat.
◆ Cut the cane 1 inch larger than the template, then soak it flat in water for about an hour.

3. Inserting the cane in the groove.
◆ Center the section of cane on the seat frame and, with a rubber mallet and a 2-inch-wide hardwood wedge, drive it into the groove at the middle of the back. The wedge will lock the cane in place.
◆ Pull the cane tightly across to the front and lock it into the groove at the middle front with a second wedge *(right)*.
◆ Insert one wedge on each side.
◆ With another wedge, drive the cane into the groove all the way around the frame. Sponge the cane if it becomes rigid.
◆ With a razor blade or a mallet and a sharp chisel, trim off any cane sticking out of the groove, removing the locking wedges as you go.

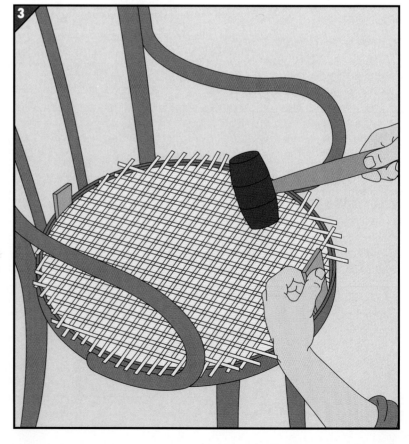

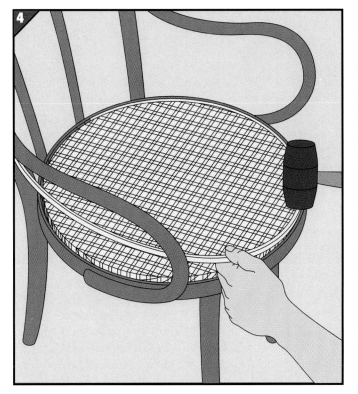

4. Inserting the spline.

◆ For a round seat, cut a length of reed spline at least 1 inch longer than the length of the groove, square its ends, and soak it in water for 20 minutes.

◆ Spread a bead of wood glue into the groove on top of the cane.

◆ Start inserting the spline at the back, tapping it lightly with a rubber mallet just enough to position it in the groove. Continue around the seat (left).

◆ When the groove is almost completely filled, lap the spline over itself, mark the overlap point, and cut it with a utility knife.

◆ With a hardwood wedge and a rubber mallet, seat the spline firmly in the groove, flush with the surface of the frame and with the ends butted. Sponge off any extruded glue and let the seat dry for at least a day.

◆ With tweezers or scissors, remove any loose cane filaments.

For a square seat, use the same basic technique, but insert a length of spline into each rail groove, mitering the ends to fit at the corners.

LACING CANE

1. Stringing the first vertical rows.

◆ Prepare the cane as described on page 52.

◆ Keeping the glossy side of the cane up, insert 4 inches of one strand of cane down through the center hole of the back rail—or, if there are an even number of holes, in the one to the left of center. Secure the 4-inch tail by fitting a caning peg or golf tee in the hole.

◆ Feed the strand of cane through the top of the corresponding hole in the middle of the front rail. Pull it snug, but not completely taut, and secure it there with a second peg.

◆ Bring the strand up through the hole to the left of the one you just threaded and move the second peg to this hole.

◆ Pull the strand across the seat, and thread it through the corresponding hole in the back rail, moving the second peg to this hole.

◆ Lace the cane, moving left and fitting the second peg in each hole as it is threaded (right). Continue until all the back holes are filled, but do not lace the corner holes. At the end of a strand, leave 4 inches hanging below the rail, and peg the end in place. Start a new strand by pegging it in the next hole as you did the first; leave these end pegs in place.

◆ Lace the right side of the seat in the same way.

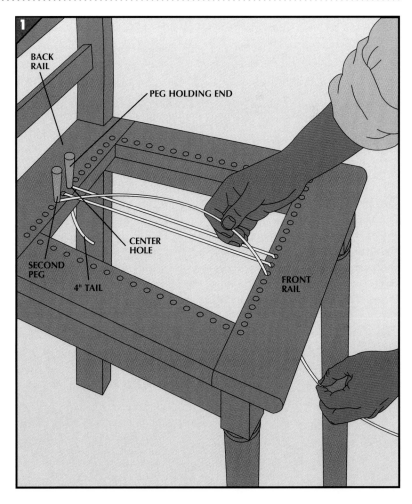

BACK RAIL

PEG HOLDING END

CENTER HOLE

SECOND PEG

4" TAIL

FRONT RAIL

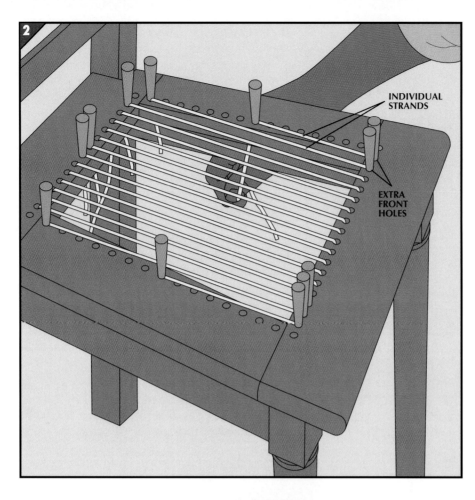

INDIVIDUAL STRANDS

EXTRA FRONT HOLES

2. Squaring the seat.

If there are no empty holes on the front rail after the holes on the back rail have been filled, go to Step 3. If empty holes remain on the front rail, peg an individual strand of cane in one of them. Keeping the strand parallel to and equally spaced from the adjacent strand, feed it down through a hole in the side rail and peg it in place. Repeat this procedure to fill the remaining front-rail holes, but leave the corner holes empty.

3. Starting the horizontal rows.

◆ Beginning at the back of the chair, peg a strand of cane in the first side hole next to the corner hole.

◆ Lace the horizontal rows as you did the vertical ones *(Step 1)*, working back and forth from side to side over the existing strands. Stop after threading cane through the last set of holes next to the front corners.

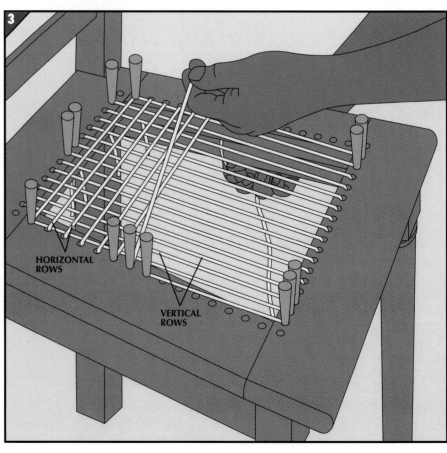

HORIZONTAL ROWS

VERTICAL ROWS

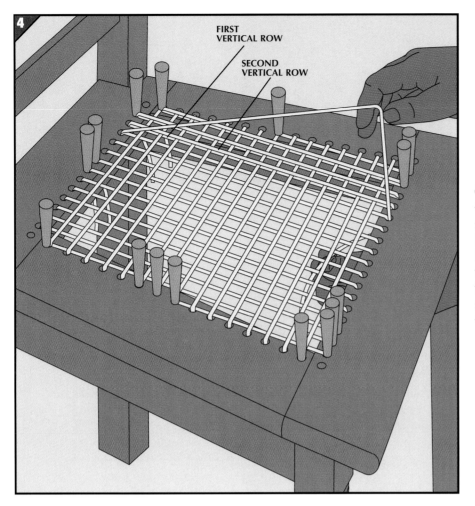

FIRST VERTICAL ROW

SECOND VERTICAL ROW

4. The second vertical rows.

◆ At the back of the seat, peg a new strand in the hole next to the right-hand corner hole. Weave strands from back to front, aligning them slightly to the right of the existing ones, and continuing until you reach the left-hand side of the chair.

◆ Fill in the short rows as in Step 2.

5. The second horizontal rows.

◆ Peg a strand of cane in the same hole in which you started the first horizontal row (Step 3).

◆ With a sponge, dampen the length of cane as well as the top and bottom of the woven seat as necessary to keep the strands pliable. Across the width of the seat, weave the cane under the first vertical row—the strand in the bottom layer—and over the second vertical row (right). Pull the excess cane through after every four or five stitches to avoid putting too many bends in it.

◆ Continue weaving until you reach the front of the seat, and peg the last strand in place.

Dampen the cane and straighten all the rows so the pairs of strands are parallel and lie close together, forming a pattern of open squares.

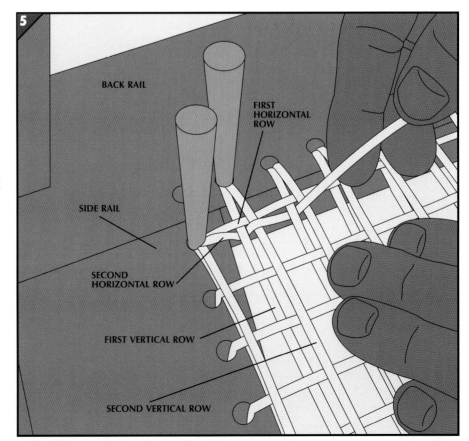

BACK RAIL

FIRST HORIZONTAL ROW

SIDE RAIL

SECOND HORIZONTAL ROW

FIRST VERTICAL ROW

SECOND VERTICAL ROW

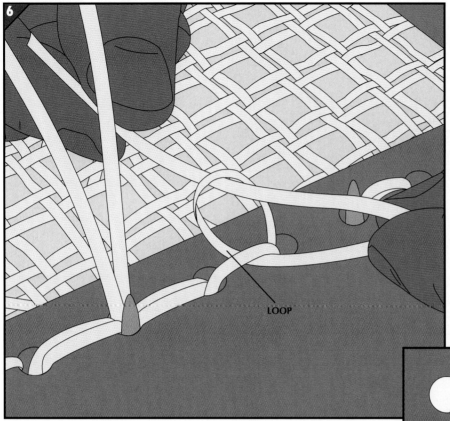

LOOP

6. Tying off the ends.
◆ Turn the chair over.
◆ Dampen the loose ends of cane with a sponge.
◆ Slip one of the ends under an adjacent strip of cane to create a loop, feeding the cane toward the outside of the seat.
◆ Pass the end through the loop *(left)* and pull the knot tight.
◆ Feed the end under the same strip *(inset)* and trim it $\frac{1}{2}$ inch from the knot.
◆ Repeat the knotting and trimming process for the remaining loose ends.

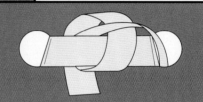

7. Lacing the first diagonal rows.
◆ Turn the chair right side up and peg a strand of cane in the left-hand corner hole at the back of the seat.
◆ Working toward the diagonally opposite corner, weave the cane over the pairs of horizontal strands and under the vertical pairs. Once you reach the opposite corner, pass the strand up through the hole in the front rail next to the corner hole and work your way toward the back of the seat, again weaving the cane under the vertical rows and over the horizontal ones *(right)*.
◆ Following this pattern, weave back and forth, keeping the rows parallel—to accomplish this, you may have to skip a hole or start two successive strands into the same hole. Continue until you reach the corner hole in the front left-hand side of the seat.
◆ Begin again at the hole in the back of the seat just to the right of the corner hole where you began, and weave diagonal rows until you reach the back right-hand corner.

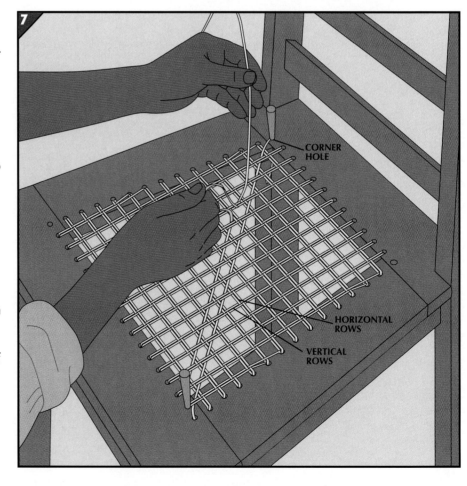

CORNER HOLE

HORIZONTAL ROWS

VERTICAL ROWS

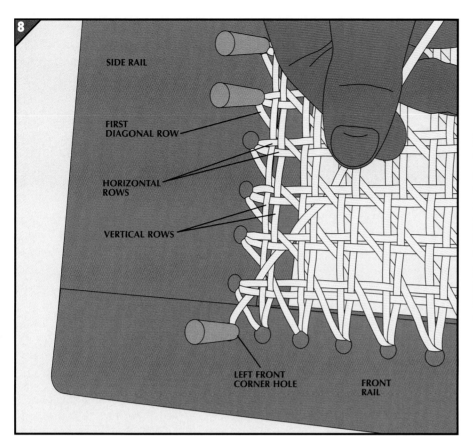

SIDE RAIL

FIRST
DIAGONAL ROW

HORIZONTAL
ROWS

VERTICAL ROWS

LEFT FRONT
CORNER HOLE

FRONT
RAIL

8. The second diagonal rows.

◆ Peg a strand of cane in the left front corner hole. Weave back and forth diagonally as you did in Step 7, weaving rows across half the seat, but this time pass under the horizontal rows and over the vertical ones *(left)*. Continue until you reach the opposite corner, then repeat the process to weave diagonal rows across the remaining half of the seat as in Step 7.
◆ Tie off the loose ends *(Step 6)*.

9. Completing the seat with binder cane.

◆ Peg a length of binder cane—cane that is one or two sizes larger than the weaving cane—in a corner hole at the back of the seat. Lay the cane across the top of the back holes.
◆ Feed a strand of weaving cane up through a hole next to a corner, leaving a tail of about 4 inches below the seat. Push it back down through the same hole over the binder cane, creating a loop to secure it.
◆ Bring the weaving cane up through the next hole and then down again, continuing to make loops through all the holes along the back of the seat until you reach the corner. Tuck the loose end of the binder cane into the corner hole, pull it taut, and peg it.
◆ Repeat the procedure with new lengths of binder and weaving cane for each side of the chair *(right)*.
◆ Tie off the weaving cane and binder cane *(Step 6)*.
◆ At each corner, tap the corner peg snugly in its hole with a mallet, then mark it flush with the surface of the seat. Remove the peg and cut it at the mark. Apply wood glue to the peg and tap it back into place. With medium-grade sandpaper, sand the top of the peg flush with the surface.

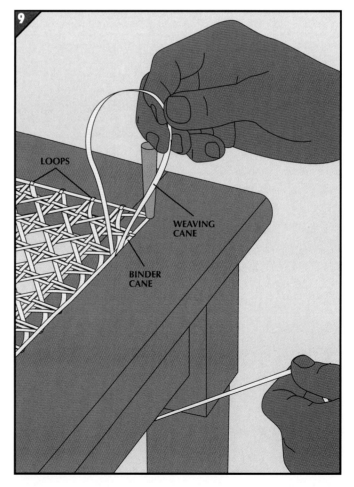

LOOPS

WEAVING
CANE

BINDER
CANE

From Touch-Ups to Refinishing

Modern wood finishes not only guard furniture against surface damage, dirt, and moisture, they also enhance the beauty of the wood. Minor blemishes in a finish can often be repaired, but extensive damage demands more drastic measures—usually stripping off the old finish and applying a new one.

Stripping a finish with chemicals →

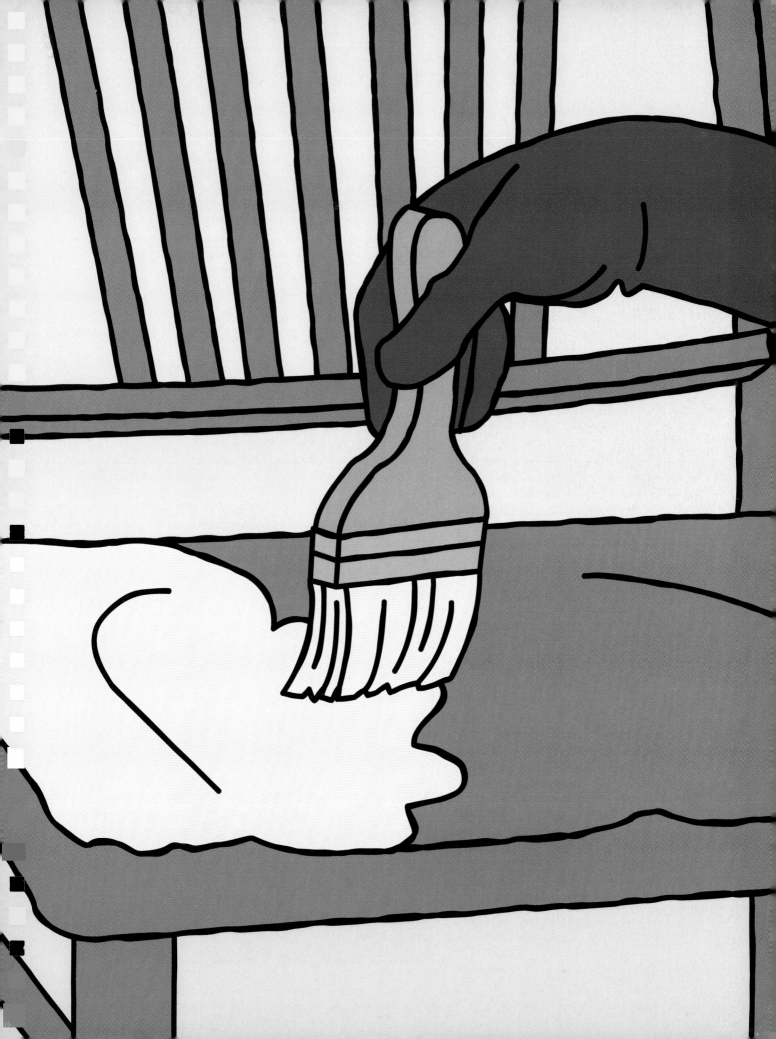

Most fine wood furniture is covered with a clear finish that allows the grain to shine through while protecting the wood against moisture, dirt, and damage. Finishes are divided into two groups: penetrating finishes such as boiled linseed oil and tung oil that soak into the wood; and surface finishes, including varnish, shellac, lacquer, and water-base finishes. Each type has unique characteristics *(pages 78-79)*.

Cleaning: The first step in restoring a finish is to clean it. The simplest cleaner is laundry detergent mixed with warm water. Before using it, however, treat a small, inconspicuous part of the surface, as water may cloud some finishes. Do not soak the wood, and rinse and dry it thoroughly. To remove deep grime or wax buildup, use mineral spirits.

Eliminating Blemishes: Any clear finish can be repaired with a range of simple techniques *(charts, pages 67-68)*. These include buffing with abrasives and filling minor scratches with furniture polishes or touch-up sticks. A more involved technique for fixing deep scratches or burns, explained in detail on page 69, is to melt a stick of wax or shellac into the depression with a hot knife. Shellac sticks are more durable than wax, but are trickier to apply.

A method of last resort for generalized damage to shellac or lacquer finishes is to soften and respread the finish with a solvent. To determine whether you can employ this technique on a piece and choose the appropriate solvent, first identify the finish *(below)*.

Protecting Finishes: After repairing a finish, buff the affected area with a fine abrasive to blend it into the surrounding finish, then spread on wax or polish. A hard automotive paste wax provides the best protection and needs renewing only three or four times a year. An oil-base polish such as lemon oil imparts a luster, but must be renewed about once a week. Avoid repeated applications of polishes containing ammonia—they can damage a finish.

⚠️ **CAUTION** *Cloths soaked in solvents or finishing products can ignite spontaneously unless stored properly; hang soaked cloths outdoors to dry, or store them in airtight metal or glass containers.*

TOOLS

Cotton-tipped swab
Single-edge
   razor blade
Burn-in knife
Artist's brush

MATERIALS

Denatured alcohol
Lacquer thinner
Mineral spirits
Wax or shellac stick
Stain and solvent
Varnish or shellac
Steel wool (4/0)
Wax or polish

IDENTIFYING LACQUER AND SHELLAC

Applying the solvent.
Dip a cotton swab in denatured alcohol and rub it on an inconspicuous spot on the furniture. If the finish softens, it is shellac. Where the finish remains unaffected, dip a second swab in lacquer thinner and rub it onto another spot. If the finish softens, it is lacquer. When the finish remains unaffected by either of these solvents, it is neither lacquer nor shellac.

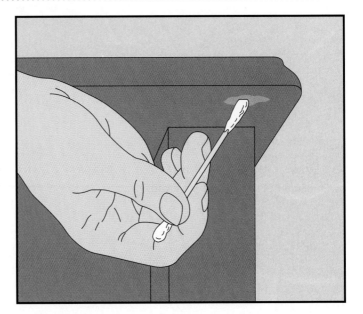

MATERIALS AND METHODS FOR REPAIRING FINISHES

Problem	Repair agent	Technique
White rings or spots	3/0 steel wool	Dip in mineral oil, rub spot with short strokes along wood grain. Wipe away excess with clean cloth.
	Rottenstone	Mix to creamy consistency with mineral oil, rub into spot with finger wrapped in clean cloth. Wipe off excess with damp rag; dry with soft cloth.
	3/F pumice	Mix to creamy consistency with mineral oil, rub spot gently along wood grain with clean cloth. Wipe off excess with damp cloth; dry with soft cloth.
	Denatured alcohol (for shellac) or lacquer thinner (for lacquer)	Wet a small lint-free pad with solvent; wring out. Stroke damaged area, remoistening pad as necessary until spot disappears.
Minor scratch	Furniture polish	Apply to entire surface with clean cloth; rub well into scratch; buff with soft cloth.
	Colored furniture polish	Rub into scratch with cotton swab; then, if desired, apply to entire surface with clean cloth.
	Furniture dye	Apply to scratch with brush or felt-tipped applicator; wipe away excess with clean cloth.
	Wax touch-up stick	Rub into depression to fill it. Wipe away excess with clean cloth.
Deep scratch	Wax or shellac burn-in stick	Melt into scratch *(page 69)*.
	Polyurethane varnish or enamel	With an artist's brush, fill scratch with repeated coats of finish, building it up higher than surrounding area; smooth with very fine sandpaper on a sanding block.
Small burn	Wax or shellac burn-in stick	Clean out all charred material with a shop knife. Melt in wax or shellac *(page 69)*.
Small chip in finish	Polyurethane varnish or enamel	With an artist's brush, fill chip with repeated coats of finish, building it up higher than surrounding area; smooth with very fine sandpaper on a sanding block.

Remedies for damage.
The chart above lists materials and techniques for repairing minor defects commonly found on furniture finishes. The chart on page 68 deals with problems affecting the entire surface. Where more than one approach is provided, start with the first one—the gentlest—and move down the list to other treatments only if necessary.

MATERIALS AND METHODS FOR REPAIRING FINISHES

Problem	Repair agent	Technique
Stubborn wax or grease, smoky blue haze	Mineral spirits	Rub in with clean cloth, changing it as needed until all traces of material are removed.
Scuffed, dull surface, multiple light scratches	Furniture polish	Apply with clean cloth; buff with soft cloth.
	Colored furniture polish	Apply with clean cloth, working into blemish to color it; buff with soft cloth.
	3/0 steel wool	Dip in mineral oil, rub over entire surface along wood grain, focusing on scratched areas. Remove excess oil with clean cloth. Wipe with clean cloth.
	Rottenstone	Mix to creamy consistency with mineral oil. Apply with clean cloth, rubbing along wood grain, giving special attention to damaged areas. Wipe off excess mixture with damp cloth; dry with soft cloth.
	3/F pumice	Mix to creamy consistency with mineral oil and apply with clean cloth, rubbing evenly along wood grain. Wipe with damp rag; dry with soft cloth.
	Denatured alcohol (for shellac) or lacquer thinner (for lacquer)	With the surface horizontal, apply solvent with natural-bristle brush; use light strokes along wood grain until scratches have melted away.
White haze	3/0 steel wool	Dip in mineral oil, rub along wood grain in long strokes over entire surface. Remove excess with clean cloth.
	Rottenstone	Mix to creamy consistency with mineral oil. Apply with clean cloth, rubbing along wood grain. Wipe off excess with damp rag; dry with soft cloth.
	3/F pumice	Mix to creamy consistency with mineral oil and apply with clean cloth, rubbing evenly along wood grain. Wipe off excess with damp rag; dry with soft cloth.
	Denatured alcohol (for shellac) or lacquer thinner (for lacquer)	With the surface horizontal, apply solvent with natural-bristle brush; use light strokes along wood grain until haze disappears.
Crackling, alligatoring	Denatured alcohol (for shellac) or lacquer thinner (for lacquer)	With the surface horizontal, apply solvent with natural-bristle brush; use light strokes along wood grain until finish softens and cracks are filled in.

PATCHING WITH HOT WAX OR SHELLAC

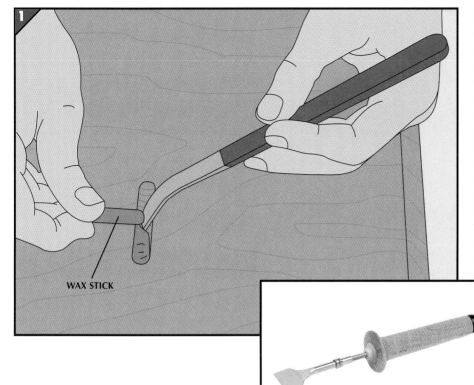

WAX STICK

1. Filling the blemish.

◆ For a burn, scrape away charred material with a single-edge razor blade or a shop knife.

◆ Clean the blemish thoroughly with a cloth soaked in mineral spirits.

◆ Heat a burn-in knife or a grapefruit knife over a gas burner or alcohol lamp, or switch on an electric burn-in knife *(photograph)*.

◆ Holding the end of a wax or shellac stick the same shade as the lightest color of the wood against the hot blade, drip the melting wax or shellac into the depression, without letting it bubble *(left)*. Reheat the blade as necessary, adding patching material to the area until it is slightly higher than the surrounding surface.

◆ When the patch is cool, pull a single-edge razor blade across the surface to level it, then smooth the patch with your finger.

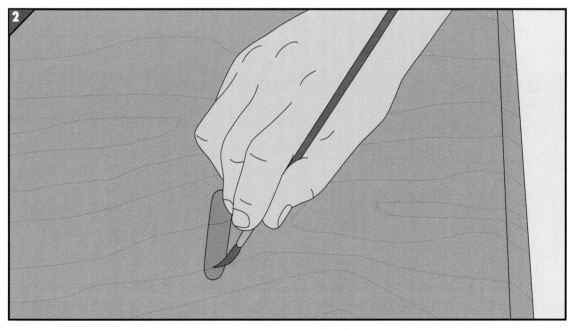

2. Matching the grain.

◆ Dilute concentrated stain with the appropriate solvent to achieve a shade that matches the grain of the wood.

◆ Dip a fine-tipped artist's brush into the stain, then wipe the bristles over paper, leaving them almost dry. With feathery strokes across the patch, blend the stain into the pattern of the surrounding wood grain *(above)*. If the lines look too crisp, smudge the color lightly with a finger or cloth.

◆ Cover the patch and surrounding surface—for a shellac-stick repair, spray a light coat of clear polyurethane or acrylic varnish; for wax-stick, brush on shellac. Let the surface dry.

◆ Buff the area with 4/0 steel wool to blend it with the texture of the finish, and wax or polish the surface.

⚠️ *Apply spray finishes in a well-ventilated room,* **CAUTION** *away from any open flame, and do not smoke.*

Stripping Down to Bare Wood

When minor repairs are insufficient, you may have to remove the finish completely. Speed and potential damage to the wood are two main considerations when choosing a method.

Chemical Stripping: The most effective chemical strippers are liquids and "semipastes" that contain methylene chloride. The paste type is easier to use because it clings to vertical surfaces. While highly effective, methylene chloride strippers give off very toxic fumes; some are flammable, and are suspected carcinogens. Although strippers containing N-methyl pyrrolidone produce fewer fumes and are less flammable, they are more toxic if they contact the skin. They also work more slowly and are more expensive than methylene chloride. To remove most finishes, more than one application of stripper will be required *(opposite)*.

So-called "no wash" strippers do not need to be removed; others must be wiped off after use with denatured alcohol. Avoid strippers that require a water wash; the water can raise the wood grain and loosen glue joints.

Removing a Finish with Heat: Heat guns are ideal for removing paint *(page 72)*, but are ineffective on lacquer and shellac.

Abrasive Techniques: Sanding or stripping attachments for electric drills *(page 72)* or power sanders used with coarse, open-coat sandpaper remove finishes rapidly; apply light pressure only to avoid gouging the surface. Do not use on fine furniture and veneers.

⚠ **CAUTION** *Do not use chemical strippers if you are pregnant. Follow product label directions, and wash your hands after use, even if you wear gloves. Work outdoors where possible. A non-flammable stripper can be used indoors provided the area is ventilated with window fans; do not use fans with a flammable stripper. Allow stripped material to dry outdoors before disposal.*

⚠ **CAUTION** *Test surfaces painted before 1978 for lead with a kit available at hardware stores. Remove lead paint with a chemical stripper, not with heat or abrasion. Keep children and pregnant women away from the work area. Dispose of stripped material as recommended by your local health department or environmental protection office.*

 TOOLS

Natural-bristle
  paintbrush
Wide-blade
  putty knife
Heat gun

Electric drill
Flap-drum,
  sanding disk, or
  sanding drum
  attachment

 **MATERIALS**

Foil pie pans
Paint stripper
Pointed dowel

Nylon abrasive
  pad (coarse)

 **SAFETY TIPS**

When using a chemical stripper, put on neoprene gloves, goggles, and a long-sleeve shirt. Wear goggles and a respirator when removing finish with an electric drill or power sander.

1. Stripping flat surfaces.

◆ Set the piece of furniture on newspapers and place foil pie pans under the legs.
◆ With an old natural-bristle paintbrush, coat a horizontal surface evenly with the stripper *(left)*.
◆ When the finish begins to bubble and dissolve (after about 5 minutes for methylene chloride strippers), scrape it off with a wide-blade putty knife and drop the material into a can.
◆ Scrub the surface with a coarse nylon abrasive pad, working parallel to the grain, to expose the next finish layer.
◆ Continue stripping the finish one layer at a time until you reach bare wood.
◆ Brush on a final, thin coat of stripper to soften any residue. Scrape it gently with the putty knife, then scrub the piece with the abrasive pad.
◆ Turn the piece so another surface is horizontal and repeat the process. Strip all the smaller surfaces such as chair legs and rungs by patting on stripper and rubbing with the pad.

2. Cleaning out cracks and crevices.

◆ Orient the furniture so the surface is horizontal and pat on stripper.
◆ When the finish has softened, gently lift it out with a pointed dowel or a cuticle stick *(right)*, being careful not to gouge the wood. For intricate carvings, a metal nut pick and a brass-bristle brush may be helpful *(photograph)*.
◆ With a coarse nylon abrasive pad, scrub gently inside the crevices.

BRASS-BRISTLE BRUSH

NUT PICK

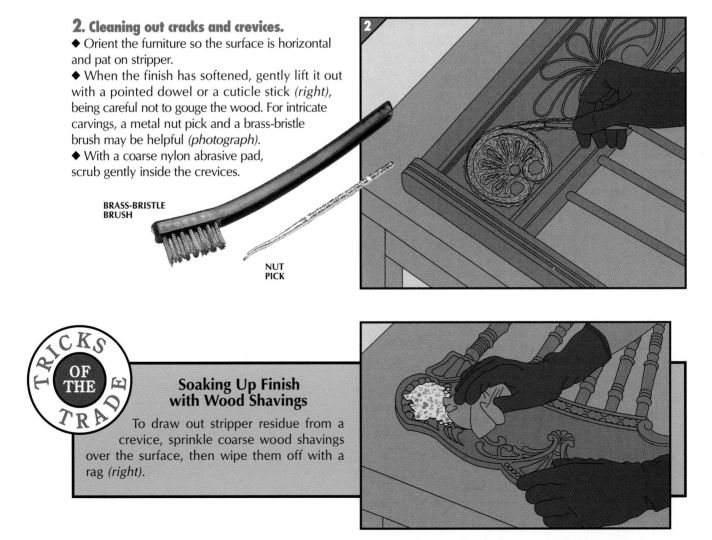

TRICKS OF THE TRADE

Soaking Up Finish with Wood Shavings

To draw out stripper residue from a crevice, sprinkle coarse wood shavings over the surface, then wipe them off with a rag *(right)*.

SOFTENING PAINT WITH HEAT

Heating the surface.
◆ Being careful not to scorch the wood, hold a heat gun or heating iron made for paint removal 2 to 4 inches from the surface.

◆ When the paint bubbles, move the heat source over to the next section and gently scrape away the paint with a wide-blade putty knife *(above)*.

◆ Keep working section by section and layer by layer until you reach bare wood.
◆ Remove any residue with a coarse nylon abrasive pad.

MECHANICAL REMOVAL

Drill attachments for contoured surfaces.
To remove paint from a contoured surface, install a flap-drum stripping attachment on an electric drill. Hold the drum about 1 inch above the surface so the sandpaper flaps will bite into the paint without leaving gouges *(right)*. Keep the drum in constant motion to avoid marring the surface.

To remove paint from the insides of concave curves, equip the drill with a small sanding drum *(photograph, left)*.

For gently contoured surfaces, install a rubber sanding disk *(photograph, right)* or a foam-padded disk with adhesive-backed paper. Hold the disk at a 30-degree angle to the surface, sweeping it back and forth.

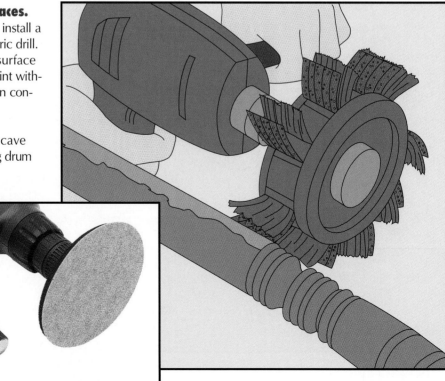

The tiniest defect in a wood surface will be visible once a finish is applied. On an antique, such blemishes are evidence of age and character, but on other pieces the wood should be sanded smooth. Work in stages, using progressively finer abrasives *(chart, right)*. For the initial sanding, power sanders are ideal, provided the surface is large and flat. Sand by hand for the final stages, and for curved or detailed surfaces.

Power Sanding: The best tools for smoothing furniture are in-line and orbital sanders, which allow precise control and reduce the possibility of gouging—a problem with belt and disk sanders. Orbital sanders work more quickly than in-line types, but leave small circular scratches on the surface.

Hand Sanding: The best tool for flat areas is a rubber-faced sanding block *(page 74)*. A long strip of sandpaper works well for round pieces, and a number of specialized tools *(page 75)* are available for reaching into tight spots.

Raising the Grain: If you plan to apply a water-base finish *(page 79)*—which will raise the wood grain—raise the fibers beforehand so they can be sanded off. To do so, wet the wood with a damp cloth so the fibers swell and rise. Let the surface dry overnight, then lightly whisk off the fibers with very fine sandpaper. To find rough spots, put your hand in an old nylon stocking and run it over the surface; if any fibers catch, sand again.

Filling Pores: Before applying a glossy clear finish to an open-pored wood such as oak, walnut, mahogany, or rosewood, first fill the pores with a wood filler that matches the color of the wood. For an exact match, buy a neutral filler and add penetrating stain or oil paint. Test the color wet; although it will lighten as the filler dries; a clear finish will darken the color again. If the wood is to be stained, do so after the final sanding, then apply the filler *(pages 76-77)*.

To use filler, thin the paste with mineral spirits to the consistency of house paint, then spread it on with an old paintbrush, pushing it into the pores. Let the filler dry until the surface is dull, then wipe it off across the grain with burlap or an old towel until it is no longer visible on the surface. Wait 24 hours, then sand it lightly with extra-fine sandpaper.

 TOOLS    **MATERIALS**

| Sanding block | Sandpaper (100-, 180-, 220-, and 240-grit) | Soft-bristle brush Cloth tape (1") |

 SAFETY TIPS

Protect your eyes with goggles when using a power sander.

A RANGE OF SANDPAPERS

Grade	Grit size	Use
Medium	80	Paint removal and rough shaping of wood
Fine	100 100 120	Initial sanding of softwoods
	150 180	Initial sanding of hardwoods
Very fine	220	Finish sanding of softwoods and most hardwoods
Extra fine	240 280	Finish sanding of very dense hardwoods
Super fine	320-360 400	Polishing between finish coats; often used wet

Choosing the right type.

A sandpaper's level of coarseness, printed on the back of the sheet, is rated by grade or by grit size—the higher the number, the finer the grit. The best papers for woodworking are covered with minerals such as garnet, silicon carbide (also called emery), or aluminum oxide. These types retain their abrasiveness much longer than ordinary flint-covered paper. There are two types of abrasive coating: closed and open. Closed-coat papers are dense with grit and cut faster, but clog quickly on softwoods or old finishes; they are best for final sandings. Open-coat papers have widely spaced grit and clog less rapidly. Use them for rough sanding and on power sanders.

Smoothing flat surfaces.

◆ To remove ridges or superficial stains, or to smooth the surface after chemical stripping, sand at a slight angle to the wood grain *(near right)*. Start with 180-grit paper; if the sanding progresses too slowly, change to 100-grit paper, then switch back to 180-grit when the surface is smoother. Continue sanding until the only roughness remaining is from the diagonal sanding scratches.

◆ Remove the scratches by sanding parallel to the grain *(far right)* with 220-grit paper.

◆ For very dense hardwoods, sand again with 240- or 280-grit.

◆ Remove the dust with a soft brush, lint-free cloth, or vacuum.

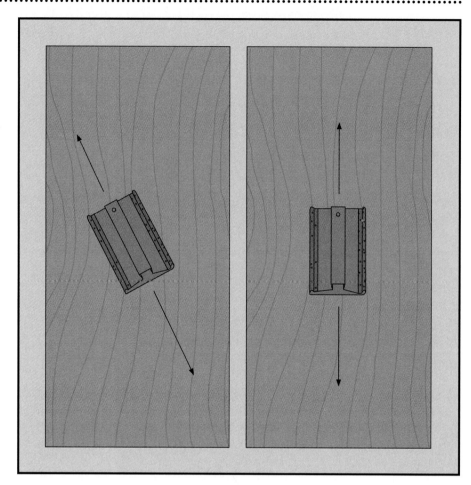

TRICKS OF THE TRADE

Checking with Light

To determine whether all the rough spots have been removed from a piece, shine a flashlight at a low angle to the surface. Examine the surface from various angles to spot any flaws.

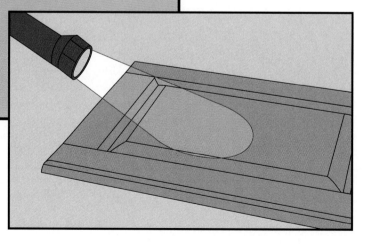

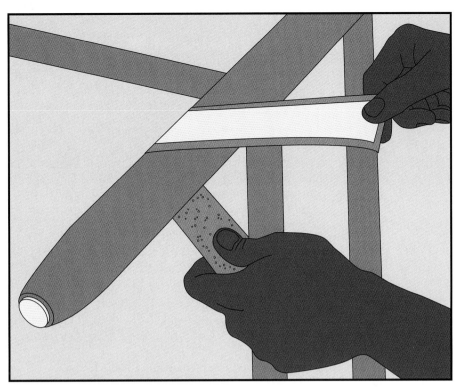

Sanding round parts.
◆ Cut a $1\frac{1}{2}$-inch-wide strip of 100-grit sandpaper, and place a length of 1-inch cloth tape against the back as reinforcement. Holding the strip at each end, draw it back and forth around the part *(above)*. Repeat the process with 220-grit paper.
◆ Sand along the length of the part with 220-grit sandpaper or, for very dense hardwoods, 240- or 280-grit.
◆ Wipe the dust off with a lint-free cloth or soft brush.

REACHING THE TIGHT SPOTS

A variety of specialized tools is available for sanding corners and curves. Abrasive cord reaches into deep grooves, sanding sticks get into tight corners, and a sanding sponge is ideal for contours. A teardrop sander will access a range of tight spots such as grooves, corners, and concave surfaces; sandpaper can even be placed inside it to smooth round parts.

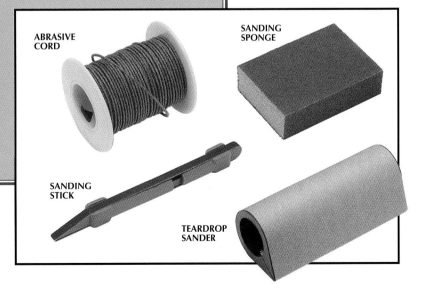

ABRASIVE CORD

SANDING SPONGE

SANDING STICK

TEARDROP SANDER

Changing the Color of Wood

With the right product, the color of wood can be altered to almost any hue. Concentrated bleaches can freshen stripped or raw wood darkened by age, or even eliminate the natural color entirely. Stains can make one wood resemble another or call attention to the grain pattern.

Bleaching Wood: Ordinary chlorine laundry bleach, diluted with water, will lighten wood, accentuating the grain. Oxalic acid, dissolved in hot water, is slightly stronger than chlorine bleach. Apply either product with a synthetic-bristle brush or a plastic-mesh scrubber and allow it to stand for 15 minutes. Repeat the process until the wood is lightened as desired, then neutralize the bleach.

For chlorine bleach, wipe on white vinegar at full strength or soap and water; for oxalic acid, use vinegar or one part ammonia in 10 parts water. Wipe the neutralizer off with a damp rag. Allow the wood to dry, then sand off the raised fibers.

With enough applications, an even stronger bleach, available as a two-part package of hydrogen peroxide and lye, can totally eliminate the natural color of wood. Apply it following the manufacturer's instructions.

Staining Wood: Penetrating stains soak into the wood and color the fibers, accentuating the grain. Non-penetrating pigment stains cover wood with a colored film and fill the wood pores, obscuring the grain.

A stain's characteristics are determined by the solvent that is used as its base *(opposite)*, and any stain can be thinned with the solvent to modify its hue.

The easiest way to apply a stain is by wiping it onto the surface *(below)*. Begin on an inconspicuous part of the piece to determine how the wood takes the stain. Any stain can be applied in multiple coats, but in the case of nonpenetrating stain, repeated coats will yield more dramatic results.

 *When using bleach, work in a well-ventilated area.* **CAUTION** *Never mix bleach with another chemical, and don't store it in metal containers.*

 TOOLS

Paintbrush
Cheesecloth

 **MATERIALS**

Sealer
Stain

SAFETY TIPS

When applying a bleach, wear rubber gloves and goggles. Put on a respirator when sanding afterward.

APPLYING A STAIN

Wiping on the stain.

◆ With a paintbrush or rag, coat all exposed end grain on the furniture with sealer; use shellac for water- or oil-base stains, and oil-base wood conditioner for alcohol-base products.
◆ With cheesecloth folded into a square or a sponge, wipe the stain on the surface; use broad strokes with the grain, pressing lightly to force the stain into the wood pores. On vertical surfaces, work from the bottom up to prevent runs *(right)*. Cover one small area at a time. Immediately wipe high spots on carved areas to lighten them, if desired, emphasizing their contours.
◆ If the color is too dark, wipe the surface using a cloth dampened with the appropriate solvent.
◆ With a nonpenetrating stain, wait until the surface is dull, then wipe away the excess with a dry cloth. With a penetrating stain, allow the stain to soak into the wood.
◆ Apply additional coats in the same way.

SELECTING A STAIN

Stain Type	Solvent	Use	Advantages	Disadvantages	Application
Penetrating	Water	All woods.	Inexpensive and easy to mix; easy to handle; broad range of colors; will not fade or bleed.	Raises wood grain; needs 24-hour drying time; not ready-mixed; not widely available.	Raise the grain and sand before application (page 73). Apply with brush or sponge; wipe off excess.
	Alcohol	All woods, but best on close-grained ones such as maple, beech, birch.	Does not raise grain; extremely fast-drying (10 to 15 minutes); available ready-mixed.	Fades in direct sunlight; application with a spray gun takes practice and experience.	Spray over small areas so overlapping areas are wet.
	Oil	Coarse-grained woods such as mahogany, oak, rosewood, walnut.	Does not raise grain; easy to use; rich tones; long lasting.	Saturates softwoods quickly, producing zebra effect; hard to remove. Will bleed through varnish unless coated with a sealer such as shellac.	Brush or wipe evenly with no overlaps. Wipe off before it sets, let dry for 24 hours.
Nonpenetrating	Oil	Close-grained woods such as birch, cherry, maple.	Disguises inexpensive woods and makes different woods look the same. Lightens coarse-grained woods and tones down grain that has uneven color distribution.	Darkens soft, porous woods; does not take well on hardwoods; accentuates dents and scratches.	Stir well before and during use. If using more than one can, premix to ensure even color. Wipe on, wait until surface dulls, wipe off.
	Varnish, shellac, or lacquer	Inexpensive woods.	Fills, colors, and adds gloss in one step.	Almost completely obscures grain; not a high-quality finish.	Apply like varnish (page 80).

An assortment of stains.
Penetrating stains contain a dye dissolved in water, alcohol, or oil. Nonpenetrating stains contain a pigment suspended in oil or a clear finish. Some products are a mixture of both and may also contain a sealer that prevents the stain from bleeding into the finish that will be overlaid. The choice of a stain depends on the type of wood to be colored and on its ease of application. Oil-base stains are generally the easiest to work with and, on hardwoods, yield the most uniform results.

Protecting Furniture with a Clear Coating

The traditional way to protect and complement fine wood furniture is with a clear finish. Most products fall into one of the six categories opposite, and they are applied in a variety of ways. For best results, work in an area with no dust, little humidity, and even lighting.

Lacquer: Lacquer is usually applied as a spray. Brush-on lacquers are available, but they have a tendency to show brush strokes. For spot repairs, lacquer can be sprayed on from an aerosol can. Finishing an entire piece, however, is usually done with a compressed-air gun—a tricky procedure for an amateur, requiring a specially designed spray booth to isolate the potentially explosive spray from sparks or flames, and exhaust the fumes outdoors.

Shellac, Varnish, and Water-Base Finishes: These products can all be applied with a brush and are built up in layers *(page 80)*. Choose a brush with chisel edges (where the center bristles are longer than the outer ones) and with bristles that are tapered. For finishes with a water base, use synthetic-bristle brushes. With shellac or varnish, either natural- or synthetic-bristle brushes are fine.

To avoid contaminating a supply of finish with dust, work with small amounts, pouring one batch at a time into a clean coffee can. To avoid slopping too much liquid on the surface, punch or drill holes near the rim of the can and twist a length of heavy wire through the holes; after dipping the bristles into the finish, strike the brush gently on the wire.

After each coat of finish dries, sand the surface and remove all dust with a tack rag *(below)* before applying the next coat.

The water in water-base products raises the grain of the wood, so you must dampen the wood and sand off the raised fibers *(page 73)* before applying the finish.

Oil Finishes and Wax: Oil finishes are the easiest to apply; they are simply wiped on *(page 81)*. Paste wax or beeswax can be rubbed on and buffed *(page 81)* as a finish, or applied over another finish to provide additional protection. Paste wax is tougher and easier to apply—beeswax must be heated.

⚠ **CAUTION** *Finishing products containing oil or solvents are flammable. Work in a well-ventilated area away from open flames, and do not smoke. To eliminate the risk of spontaneous combustion, let finish-soaked rags dry outdoors before disposing of them, or store them in an airtight container.*

 TOOLS

Tack rag
Paintbrush

 **MATERIALS**

Coffee can
Heavy wire
Finishing product
    and appropriate
    solvent
Scrap wood and
    nails for props
Steel wool
    (3/0, 4/0)
Sandpaper
    (320-grit)
Soft cloths

 **SAFETY TIPS**

When working with a finish or solvent, put on goggles and nitrile gloves.

TRICKS OF THE TRADE

Making a Tack Rag

When sanding a piece of furniture between coats of finish, you'll need a tack rag to pick up the dust. For a water-base finish, simply dampen a cloth with water and wring it out well. In the case of solvent-base finishes, you can buy one at a hardware store, or you can make your own from a 24-inch square of cheesecloth. Sprinkle the cloth with a few teaspoons of mineral spirits and a few drops of varnish. Wring the cloth until it begins to feel sticky. Add mineral spirits and varnish when it loses its tack. Store the rag in an airtight container to eliminate the risk of spontaneous combustion.

In addition to their application methods, clear finishes differ in their appearance and in the protection they afford. All products darken wood slightly, particularly dark wood, giving it a richer color *(photograph)*. Varnishes and oil finishes are available for both indoor and outdoor use, while shellac, lacquer, wax, and water-base finishes are intended for indoor furniture only.

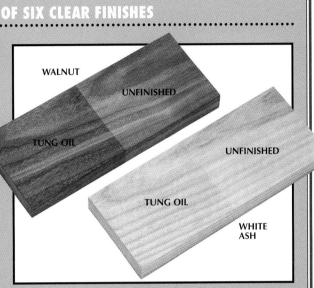

Lacquer: Lacquer hardens on a surface when its solvent content evaporates. Sprayed lacquer dries mirror smooth, but you can tone down the surface shine to a sheen by rubbing it with very fine steel wool. A lacquer finish provides good resistance to wear and moisture.

Shellac: Shellac is available ready to use, or as flakes or buttons that must be dissolved in denatured alcohol. White shellac is clear and colorless; orange shellac imparts a slight tint to wood, but is somewhat more resistant to moisture. Though shellac will protect wood from moisture, dampness discolors it and alcohol dissolves it. Shellac can be applied as a base coat between an oil stain and varnish to prevent the stain from bleeding into the finish. A shellac finish can be rubbed with fine steel wool or polished to modify its gloss.

Varnish: The term "varnish" includes a diverse group of clear, tough, extremely durable finishes. Those best suited for wood furniture are alkyd-resin, phenolic-resin, and polyurethane varnishes. Both alkyd- and phenolic-resin varnishes give a warm, glowing tone to wood. Phenolic-resin varnish, commonly labeled "spar varnish" or "marine varnish," has a tendency to darken or yellow. Especially formulated for outdoor use, it remains slightly flexible to accommodate the shrinking and swelling of the wood it covers. Prized for its extreme durability and moisture resistance, polyurethane varnish produces a high-gloss finish, but successive coats won't bond well unless the surface is well sanded between coats.

Wax: Either paste wax or beeswax can be applied as a clear finish. Both afford some protection against scuffing, but neither helps against heat, water, or solvents. If applied to a bare softwood, wax precludes later refinishing because it cannot be removed from the wood pores.

Paste wax can be applied over other clear finishes as a buffer against grime and wear. Since wax will yellow eventually, it must be removed once or twice a year and renewed.

Oils: Valued for their soft sheen and subtle beauty, rubbing oils are certainly the easiest clear finishes to apply. Tung oil and boiled linseed oil are the most commonly used on furniture. They penetrate the pores of the wood and, with repeated applications, gradually form a clear, hard film on the wood. Oil finishes can easily be touched up or recoated, but are not particularly durable and have virtually no resistance to moisture.

Water-Base Finishes: These products create a very scuff-resistant finish, which is also resistant to water, heat, and solvents. With water as their primary component, these products are not flammable and their fumes are not as toxic as those of solvent-base finishes.

1. Brushing on the first coat.

◆ Dilute phenolic and alkyd varnish with an equal part of mineral spirits, and premixed shellac with an equal part of denatured alcohol. Dilute polyurethane varnish and water-base finishes only if recommended by the manufacturer.

◆ Prop up the furniture so the largest surface is horizontal. To treat the lower part of the legs, build props from scrap wood as shown to hold the piece above the surface.

◆ For varnish, dip the brush to half the length of the bristles and apply a heavy load of finish to a small area, working across the grain. Without reloading the brush, go back over the area, brushing with the grain *(right)*. To smooth the finish, lightly run the tip of a nearly dry brush, held almost perpendicular to the surface, over the area with the grain. For shellac and water-base finishes, apply a thin coat, starting from the middle of a surface and working toward the edges; lift the brush slightly when you reach an edge to avoid pooling finish on the adjacent surface.

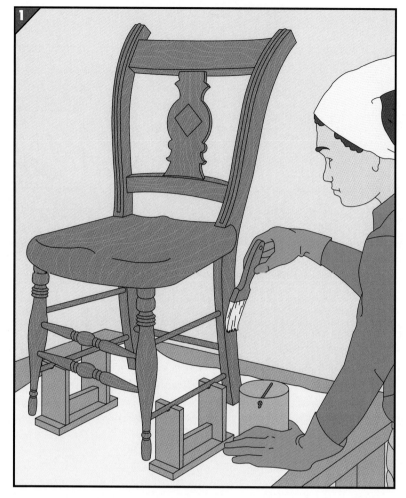

2. Sanding between coats.

◆ Let the finish dry as recommended on the label, then press your thumb against the surface and wipe the area with a soft cloth; if the thumbprint remains, more drying time is needed.

◆ With 3/0 steel wool—or 320-grit sandpaper for a water-base finish—rub the surface lightly and evenly with the grain *(left)*. At the edges, take care not to cut all the way through the finish.

◆ When the surface is smooth and free of imperfections, remove sanding dust with a tack rag *(page 78)*.

◆ Apply additional coats in the same way as the first one *(Step 1)*, but use undiluted finish. Let each coat dry and sand it smooth before applying the next. For a very deep finish, you can apply as many as six coats.

◆ Allow the final coat to dry for 24 hours, then polish the finish to a soft sheen with 4/0 steel wool or, for a glossier look, with 6/0 steel wool.

RUBBING ON TUNG OIL OR LINSEED OIL

Wiping on the oil.

◆ Pour undiluted tung oil on the furniture, and rub it over the surface with a soft lint-free cloth.

◆ Allow the oil to stand for a few minutes, then wipe away any excess and let the wood dry overnight.

◆ Apply additional coats in the same way.

◆ To add sheen to the final coat, rub the surface with 4/0 steel wool.

◆ To apply boiled linseed oil, mix the oil with an equal part of mineral spirits and rub it over the surface with a soft cloth.

◆ Continue to apply oil until the surface will not absorb any more. Then wipe away the excess and allow the wood to dry for two weeks before use.

◆ Apply additional coats as desired.

◆ Buff the surface with a dry cloth.

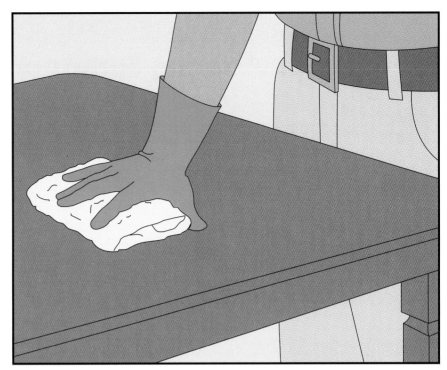

WAXING FURNITURE

Applying paste wax.

◆ For cream wax, rub a thin layer on the surface with a soft cloth (left).

◆ Wait until the wax film turns dull, then wipe off the excess with a clean cloth.

◆ Apply a second coat of wax in the same way.

◆ Wait the recommended time, then buff the surface with a soft cloth, or use an electric drill fitted with a fleece buffing pad (photograph).

To apply a hard wax, knead a lump to soften it, then wrap the lump in a soft cloth and rub it over the surface to deposit a thin film of wax. Buff the surface as for cream wax.

4 Reupholstering Furniture

Few improvements change the countenance of a room more dramatically or yield bigger dividends in comfort than newly upholstered furniture. The basic tools and procedures illustrated on the following pages have been used for centuries by fine craftsmen to upholster and reupholster furniture.

Stripping cambric from a chair →

Reupholstering furniture requires some special tools and supplies, available from hardware stores, upholstery-supply outlets, and mail-order houses. Besides the items shown below and on page 86, and those listed in the chart opposite, you will need a few others.

Tools: For sewing the fabric, equip your sewing machine with a zipper foot. Marking pencils made specifically for fabric or tailor's chalk are best for marking cutting lines on the material. Also have on hand a craft knife, a rubber mallet, and sturdy scissors—ideally 10-inch upholstery shears—wood glue, and spray adhesive. Purchase heavy-gauge dressmaker's pins to fasten together the pieces before sewing them by machine.

Materials: In addition to the upholstery fabric, other fabrics—as well as springs, webbing, and twine—are used in building up the inner structure of the piece. You can purchase new stuffing, but in some cases it is better to reuse the original stuffing if it is in good shape—either to preserve the authenticity of an old piece, or because it is already shaped to the furniture's contours.

Welt—the trim that outlines some seams—can be made by covering welt cord with upholstery fabric, or it can be bought ready-made in a suitable color. Matching buttons can also be purchased, or a professional uphosterer can fashion them from your fabric. Finally, you will need sturdy thread for stitching—by hand and machine.

Fasteners.

Upholstery fasteners come in several forms, depending on their use. Useful tack sizes are No. 3, for one or two layers of fabric or burlap; No. 4, for tack tape, tack strips, and padding; and No. 6, for more than two layers. For webbing, No. 14 tacks can be used, but special webbing nails are less likely to split the wood. Ornamental tacks—available with brass, silver, colored, and hammered heads—are used to decorate trim. Cardboard tack tape, with or without embedded tacks, or flexible metal tack strips are used where they can be concealed inside a fabric fold.

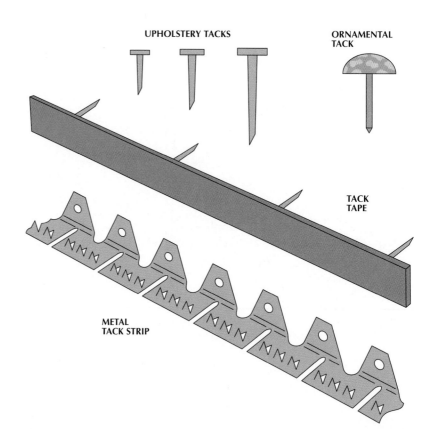

UPHOLSTERY TACKS

ORNAMENTAL TACK

TACK TAPE

METAL TACK STRIP

UPHOLSTERY SUPPLIES

Material	Use	Recommended type
Burlap	Separates springs from stuffing; covers webbing when no springs are used	10- to 12-ounce weight
Buttons	Decorate seat backs	Fabric-covered upholstery buttons
Cambric	Covers the underside of chairs, keeping out dust	Glazed, tightly woven
Decking	Covers chair seats under loose cushions	Denim, cotton duck, or flannel
Edge roll	Prefabricated padding for front edge of chair seats	Burlap covered, $1\frac{1}{2}$" in diameter
Ornamental gimp or double welt	Covers tacks holding fabric to edge of frames	Style and color appropriate for furniture
Padding	Covers wood-frame surfaces to cushion their edges; covers stuffing and gives it shape	1" thick sheets of long-staple cotton over rubberized hair stuffing; polyester batting over foam stuffing; either type over other types of stuffing
Spring twine	Ties down coil springs	Polyester or jute
Stitching twine	Secures stuffing to burlap, burlap to springs, springs to webbing; also used to attach buttons	Nylon
Stuffing	Covers springs and seat backs; fills cushions	Polyurethane foam in either bulk form or rolls; rubberized hair in rolls; felt; pressed coconut fibers; down for cushions
Webbing	Tacked across bottom of frame to serve as a foundation for springs or padding	Tightly woven bands of jute or polyester $3\frac{1}{4}$" to 4" wide—a red stripe near the edge indicates the best quality; rubber or steel
Welt	Ready-made fabric-covered cord sewn into seams	Available in many colors and several sizes to suit upholstery fabrics.
Welt cord	Soft cotton cord to be covered with fabric	$\frac{1}{4}$" or $\frac{5}{32}$" in diameter

IMPLEMENTS FOR STRIPPING AND ATTACHING FABRIC

Specialized upholstery tools.

For removing fabric from upholstered furniture, you'll need a claw chisel, staple remover, or ripping chisel, depending on the fasteners securing the old fabric.

For attaching fabric, a wider range of tools is required. Use a webbing stretcher to fasten webbing. The traditional tool for attaching new fabric is a magnetized tack hammer. For large projects, an electric staple gun speeds this work but, should you make a mistake, the staples are difficult to remove without ripping the fabric. Even with a staple gun, you still need tacks and a hammer to pin the fabric to the frame before stapling. You will also need specialized pins and needles for sewing fabric and springs.

Staple remover.
The slotted tip is designed to reach under staples and lift them out.

Webbing stretcher.
The stretcher's sharp spikes and rubber tread grip webbing to pull it tight across the frame.

Claw chisel.
Also called a tack lifter, this tool has a V-shaped notch at its tip and is curved to provide leverage for prying out tacks.

Tack hammer.
The head has one magnetic end for picking up tacks and a nonmagnetic end for driving them.

Ripping chisel.
For removing very stubborn tacks and staples, the chisel is held against the fastener and struck with a rubber mallet to free the fastener.

Electric staple gun.
These guns easily drive long staples through heavy materials and into wood frames.

Curved upholstery needle.
A 3" to 4" curved needle is used to blind-stitch fabric and fasten burlap to springs or stuffing to burlap.

Upholstery pin.
Sturdy enough to hold heavy materials, these pins are used to pin fabric to the furniture and have pierced heads for easy removal.

Upholstery needle.
A 10" straight needle with points at both ends pierces webbing to attach springs. This version—or one with a point at only one end—goes through padding to attach buttons.

The most common problem with an upholstered chair or sofa is a sagging seat, often a result of loose webbing or springs. The springs are typically supported by crisscrossed strips of webbing, which are usually made of jute, although some seats may have rubber or steel webbing.

The repair techniques in this section work on sofas as well as chairs. Refer to the illustrations on pages 91 and 92 for identifying the parts of a typical upholstered chair.

Seats with Jute Webbing: Turn the chair upside down and remove the cambric covering to expose the webbing and springs *(below)*. If springs are broken, badly out of line, or popping through the fabric either above or below them, rebuild the base *(pages 94-98)*. In cases where the springs are intact but the webbing is loose or worn, reinforce the seat by reattaching any loose springs *(page 88)*, filling in cracks

or holes in the frame with wood putty or glue, and adding new webbing over the existing strips *(page 89)*. Where the edge of the frame has been weakened by too many tack holes, fasten the new webbing to the side of the frame, leaving the ends unfolded to avoid bulges under the fabric cover.

Seat Variations: Rubber webbing, common in Danish modern furniture, can be replaced if broken *(page 90)*. For a chair with sagging steel webbing, obtain a special tool from a professional upholsterer to restretch it.

In modern chairs, the seat is often supported by zigzag-shaped metal springs with no webbing. If springs have worked loose from each other, retie them from the bottom, or from the top if you are recovering the chair *(page 99)*. Where a spring has come loose from the frame, take the seat apart from the top and reattach the spring.

 TOOLS

Pliers	Curved
Claw chisel	needle (4")
Staple	Scissors
remover	Tack hammer
Ripping chisel	Webbing
Rubber mallet	stretcher

 **MATERIALS**

Nylon stitching	Jute webbing
twine	Cambric
Upholstery tacks	Rubber webbing
(Nos. 3, 14)	and clips

SAFETY TIPS

Protect your eyes with goggles when hammering upholstery tacks.

GETTING AT THE WEBBING

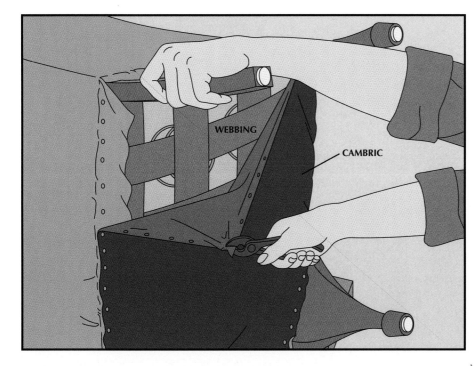

Stripping off the cambric.
◆ Place the chair on its back or side on a worktable.
◆ With pliers, grasp the cambric—the fabric on the underside of the chair—at one corner and pull it diagonally toward the opposite corner, stripping it off the frame *(left)*.
◆ Remove all the fasteners from the bottom of the frame, using a claw chisel for tacks and a staple remover for staples; pull stubborn fasteners with a ripping chisel.

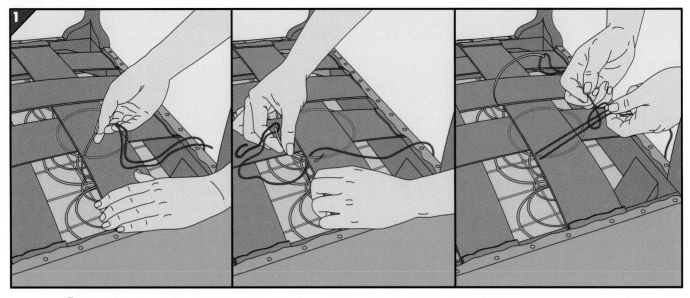

1. Making the first stitch.

Anchor a loose spring with four stitches of nylon stitching twine spaced equally around its circumference so they form a square. Locate the first stitch so the last one will fall as close as possible to the next spring to be resewn.

◆ Clip away any bits of loose or broken twine tying the springs to the existing webbing.

◆ Thread a 4-inch curved needle with a 3-foot length of twine, then push the needle down through the webbing inside the spring's coil *(above, left)* and bring it up through the webbing outside the coil *(above, center)*.

◆ Tie a slipknot in the twine *(above, right)*, and make the knot fast against the webbing.

2. Making subsequent stitches.

◆ Take the second stitch at the adjoining corner of the square, plunging the needle down through the webbing inside the coil and bringing it up outside the coil.

◆ Lock this stitch by slipping the needle under the twine between the two stitches *(right)*.

◆ Take the third and fourth stitches in the same way.

◆ Repeat the procedure with the next loose spring. If the two springs are adjacent, do not cut the twine—continue using it to anchor the spring; if not, cut the twine, tie a knot, and resew the second spring with a new length.

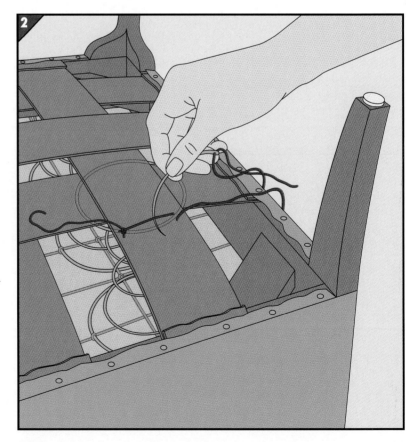

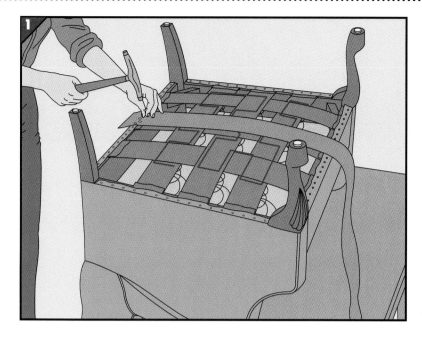

1. Placing the first strip.

◆ Unroll the webbing and position it over the center strip of the existing webbing so it overlaps the back seat rail by 1 inch.

◆ With a tack hammer, drive a No. 14 upholstery tack through the end of the webbing into the back rail.

◆ Drive four additional tacks through the webbing in a staggered pattern *(left)*. If the folded edge of the existing webbing falls slightly in from the edge of the rail, try to place some of the tacks in the narrow strip of wood beyond the webbing. Otherwise, drive the tacks through the old webbing.

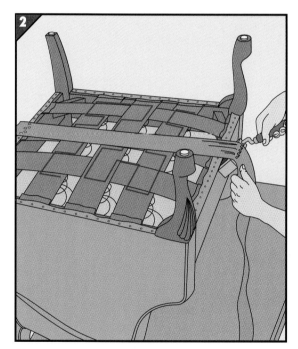

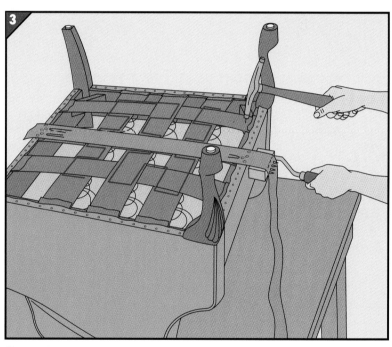

2. Stretching the webbing.

◆ Holding a webbing stretcher against the front seat rail at a 45-degree angle, pull the strip down over the teeth of the stretcher *(above)*.

◆ Push down on the handle of the stretcher until it is horizontal.

3. Tacking the webbing to the front rail.

◆ Holding the stretcher with one hand, pick up a tack with the magnetic end of the hammer. Position the hammer about 6 inches above the webbing strip and, with a sharp blow, drive the tack down through the center of webbing and partway into the rail.

◆ Flip the hammer over and drive the tack all the way into the wood with the nonmagnetic end.

◆ Tack both edges of the strip in the same way, then drive in two intermediate tacks in a staggered pattern *(above)*. Remove the stretcher and cut the webbing from the roll, leaving a 1-inch overhang.

◆ Fasten additional webbing strips across the underside of the seat in the same way. Then weave in strips from side to side, starting with the middle strip, stretching and fastening them to the rails.

◆ Fold back each overhanging end and fasten it with five more tacks.

MAKING A CAMBRIC DUST COVER

FOLD LINE

Attaching new cambric.
◆ Cut a piece of cambric large enough to overlap the bottom of the chair frame on all sides by $\frac{1}{2}$ inch.
◆ Along each edge of the cambric, fold under $\frac{3}{4}$ inch of the material. Position the cambric on the frame so the fold line falls $\frac{1}{4}$ inch inside the edge of the frame on all four sides. With No. 3 upholstery tacks, fasten the cambric temporarily to the frame at the midpoint of each seat rail, beyond the webbing.
◆ Working from the middle toward the end of each rail, tack the cambric permanently to the frame at 1-inch intervals *(left)*, cutting and fitting it around the legs *(page 111)*.

REPLACING RUBBER WEBBING

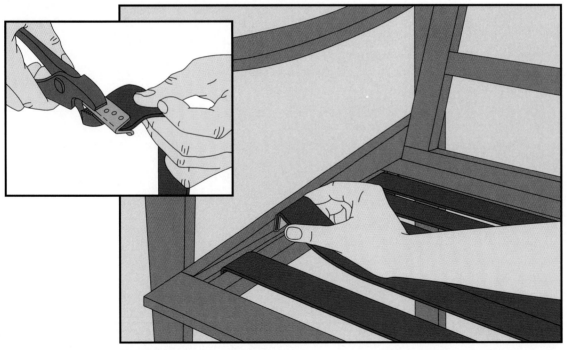

Fastening new end clips.
◆ Slide the broken band of rubber webbing out of its grooves in the seat rails.
◆ Measure the old band and, with heavy scissors, cut a new one $\frac{1}{2}$ inch shorter.
◆ Place a webbing clip over one end of the new band and pinch the jaws closed with pliers *(inset)*. Attach a clip to the other end of the band in the same way.
◆ Install the new band by sliding the clips into the grooves in the frame *(above)*.

Upholstered chairs and sofas are typically covered with a number of fabric sections joined together that conceal the wooden frame with its springs, webbing, and layers of padding, stuffing, and burlap *(below)*. Before recovering a piece, remove the old fabric cover and any inner layers of material in poor condition.

Stripping the Cover: Remove all the pieces carefully *(page 93)* so they can be used as patterns when you cut the new fabric. Label each piece with its location before lifting it from the chair, and note where sections are tacked to the frame or sewed together. Record the location of welt. To keep track of intricate details, you may want to draw sketches or take snapshots.

Measure the pieces to determine the amount of new fabric you'll need. Add extra material for welt, if you are making your own; a yard is usually enough. Figure an additional 20 percent more for matching patterns, centering dominant design elements, or positioning napped fabrics.

Removing Inner Layers: To recover the chair, the layers of padding and burlap must be removed from the outside of the chair. Padding, stuffing, and burlap need to be removed from the inside of the chair only if you plan to restructure the back or seat *(pages 94-99)*. Otherwise, these layers can be left in place and a layer of new padding added before the final cover is attached in place.

On some antique pieces, you may need to remove a piece of muslin under the fabric cover to reach the inner layers.

Inspecting the Frame: Once you have removed the cover and inner layers, check the condition of the frame and make necessary repairs. Refinish any exposed parts of the arms and legs, if desired.

TOOLS

Pliers
Claw chisel
   or staple remover

Seam ripper
Scissors
Screwdriver
Ripping chisel
Rubber mallet

SAFETY TIPS

When removing an old upholstery cover, wear goggles to protect your eyes from flying tacks.

Anatomy of an upholstery cover.
The fabric sections shown at right are common to most fully upholstered chairs, although not all chairs have wings. The inside fabric sections are tacked or stapled to the frame. Outside pieces are hooked onto hidden tack strips joining them to adjacent pieces. The front arm covers are attached to the arm pieces with a combination of machine sewing and blind tacking.

The corded welt that outlines the seams between some of the fabric sections is machine-stitched. The cushion sections are sewn together, edged with welt, and closed with a zipper.

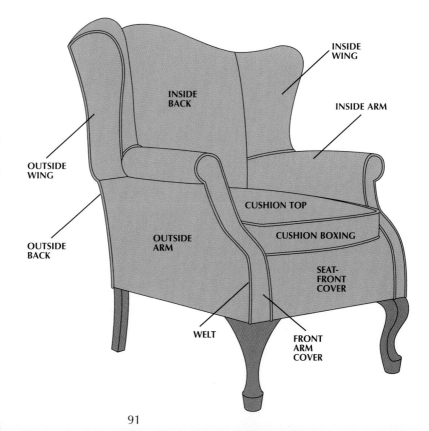

INSIDE WING
INSIDE BACK
INSIDE ARM
OUTSIDE WING
OUTSIDE BACK
OUTSIDE ARM
CUSHION TOP
CUSHION BOXING
SEAT-FRONT COVER
WELT
FRONT ARM COVER

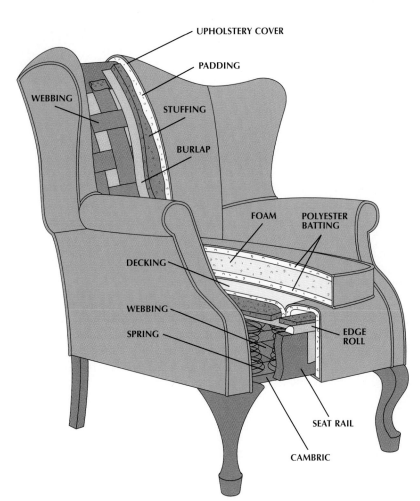

UPHOLSTERY COVER

PADDING

WEBBING

STUFFING

BURLAP

FOAM

POLYESTER BATTING

DECKING

WEBBING

SPRING

EDGE ROLL

SEAT RAIL

CAMBRIC

The inner structure.

The inside of a chair is built up in layers designed for both comfort and support. The bottom layer of the back and seat is made up of interwoven strips of webbing. In the arms, support is often provided by a panel of burlap instead of webbing.

In the seat—and, in some chairs, in the back as well—coil springs are sewn to the webbing and tied together with twine. A layer of burlap is stretched over the springs, serving as a base for the stuffing; a special burlap- or felt-covered padding strip, called an edge roll, cushions the top edge of the seat rail. A layer of padding defines the contours of the upholstery. Beneath the seat, the webbing and springs are protected by a cambric dust cover.

Although many older seat cushions contain springs, most modern cushions are stuffed with foam rubber or polyurethane foam and shaped with polyester batting. Underneath the cushion is a square of durable fabric, called decking, that covers the top of the chair seat.

The chair frame.

The frame of a piece of upholstered furniture is typically constructed of horizontal rails and vertical stiles, all hardwood, assembled with mortise-and-tenon joints or butt joints strengthened with dowels. Corner blocks are added to reinforce the joints between seat rails. The other frame pieces—arms, slats, and braces—give shape to the upholstery and provide tacking surfaces for fastening the fabric. The wings are a decorative addition to the seat back.

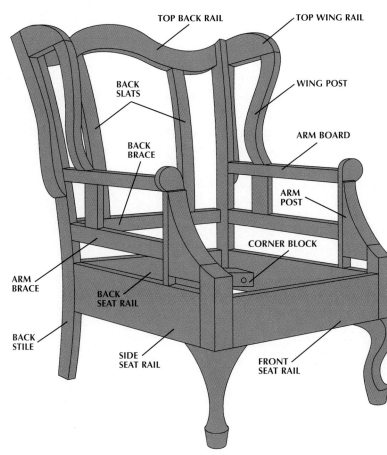

TOP BACK RAIL

TOP WING RAIL

BACK SLATS

WING POST

BACK BRACE

ARM BOARD

ARM POST

CORNER BLOCK

ARM BRACE

BACK SEAT RAIL

BACK STILE

SIDE SEAT RAIL

FRONT SEAT RAIL

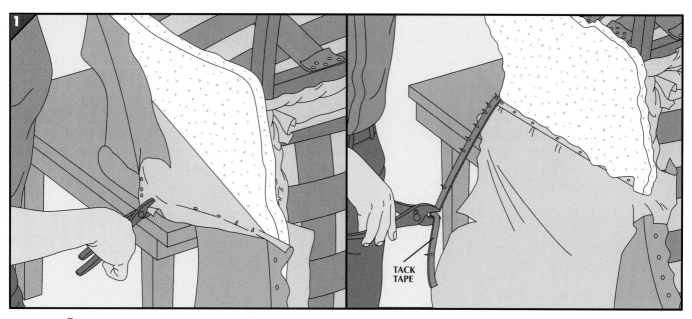

1. Stripping off the fabric.

◆ Position the chair upside down on a work surface and pull off the cambric dust cover *(page 87)*.

◆ Remove the fabric pieces in the following order: outside back and wings, outside arms, inside back and wings, inside arms and front arm cover, and finally the seat front cover and decking. For tacked-down pieces, pull down diagonally on a corner of the fabric with pliers to free it from the frame *(above, left)*. If necessary, pry out fasteners with a claw chisel or staple remover as you go to avoid tearing the fabric. If tack tape does not come free with the fabric, strip it away from the frame with pliers *(above, right)*, pulling downward to prevent tacks from flying up. For sections that have been hand-stitched to other pieces, cut the first few stitches with a seam ripper or craft knife; then rip open the rest of the seam, cutting stitches as necessary. For fabric caught in tack strips, pry the strip open with a screwdriver.

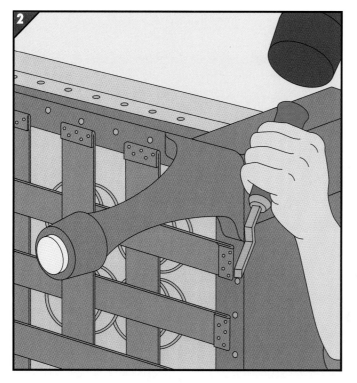

2. Clearing the frame.

◆ Lift the padding off the outside of the chair; if it is in good shape, set it aside to be put back later.

◆ Strip away the burlap on the outside of the chair as you stripped the fabric *(Step 1)*.

◆ Remove any remaining tacks or staples from the frame. Use a ripping chisel for stubborn fasteners; with the blade flat on the surface, pointed away from you and aligned with the wood grain, wedge the tip under the head of the tack and strike the handle with a rubber mallet *(left)*.

Most chair and sofa seats have either coil or zigzag springs *(below)*. If the only problem with a coil-spring seat is stretched or frayed webbing, or broken thread, you can reinforce the bottom of the seat without exposing the springs *(pages 87-89)*.

Rebuilding a Coil-Spring Seat: If springs are popping through the fabric, either above or below, or are tied together so loosely that they can easily be pushed out of alignment, you'll need to rebuild the seat. Before tearing the seat apart, mark the positions of the old webbing strips on the bottom edges of the seat rails with chalk as a guide for installing new webbing. Then, remove any padding, stuffing, and burlap, pulling tacks as necessary. (If the stuffing is in good shape, preserve it to replace later.) Cut the twine that fastens the springs at the top, and that anchors the bottoms of the springs to the webbing. Finally, take out the springs and remove the webbing by prying out the tacks holding it to the frame.

In many cases, you can reuse the old springs. However, if you want either a softer or a firmer seat, replace them with springs that are more or less springy.

To rebuild the seat, stretch a new layer of jute webbing across the seat bottom as you would to reinforce existing webbing *(page 89)*. Then install the springs *(opposite and pages 96-98)*.

Repairing Zigzag Springs: Zigzag springs do not require webbing, but they are generally fastened together with metal connectors. If the connectors have broken, the springs can be tied back together with twine *(page 99)*. In some cases, you may also need to reattach the springs to the frame.

Replacing Back Webbing: When the back of a chair loses its firmness, you will need to repair the webbing. First, strip off the burlap. It is possible to restretch loose webbing *(page 99)*, but if it is badly deteriorated, you'll need to replace the webbing in the same manner as you would for seat webbing *(page 89)*.

 TOOLS

Double-pointed
 upholstery needle
Scissors

Tack hammer
Pliers
Claw chisel
Upholstery pins
Webbing stretcher

 **MATERIALS**

Stitching twine
Double-cone
 springs

Spring twine
Upholstery tacks
 (No. 14)
Wood glue
Webbing

 **SAFETY TIPS**

Put on goggles when hammering tacks and when repairing zigzag springs.

AN ASSORTMENT OF SPRINGS

The springs in the seats of upholstered furniture may be one of three types. Most well-made furniture has springs of 9-gauge wire in a double-cone shape. Double-cone springs are rated as hard, medium, or soft: The smaller the narrowest coil in the middle of the spring, the harder the spring. If you replace springs with softer or harder ones, make sure the new springs are the same height as the old ones when compressed by hand.

Some seats have a set of single-cone springs, mounted as a unit on metal bars. If this assembly is faulty, remove it and rebuild the seat with webbing and double-cone springs.

In modern pieces, you may find flat zigzag springs, which are fastened to the frame with metal clips and to each other with wire ties.

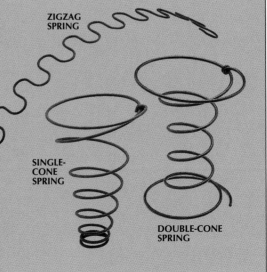

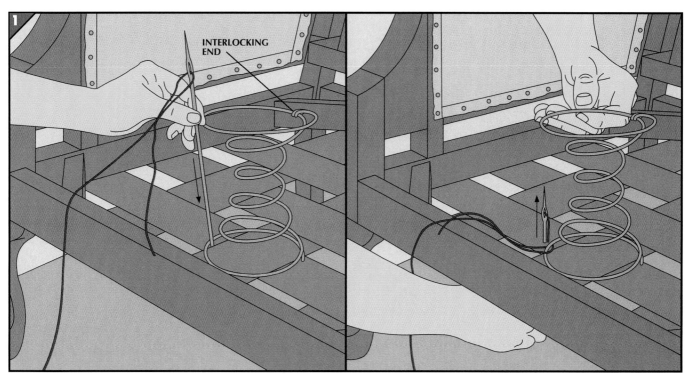

INTERLOCKING
END

1. Making the first stitch.

◆ Center the first spring over the intersection of the front and center strips of webbing; if the spring is interlocked at one end, place that end up.

◆ Thread a double-pointed needle with nylon stitching twine.

◆ Push the needle straight down through the webbing just inside the left edge of the coil *(above, left)*.

◆ Bring the needle up through the webbing on the outside of the coil *(above, right)* and pull the twine through until a 1-foot length of it is above the webbing.

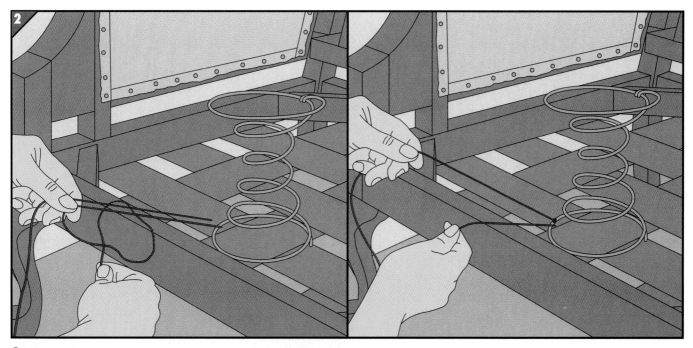

2. Anchoring the first stitch.

◆ Double the loose end over the length of twine and back through the loop in the loose end to form a slipknot *(above, left)*.

◆ Tighten the knot against the coil *(above, right)* and trim the short end.

◆ Push the needle down, outside the coil, through the hole in the webbing.

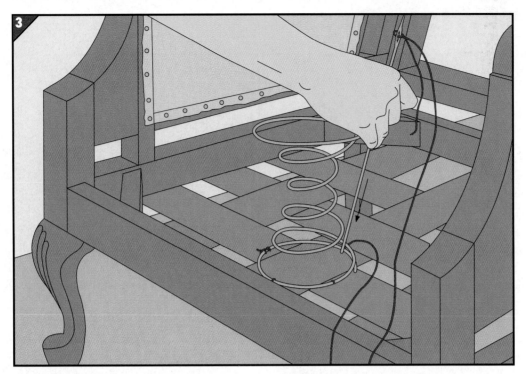

3. Making the remaining stitches.

◆ Make a second stitch at the front of the coil, pushing the needle up through the webbing inside the coil and back down outside the coil.

◆ Make a third stitch at the right edge of the coil in the same way as the second.

◆ Make a fourth stitch at the back of the coil, this time pushing the needle up through the webbing outside the coil, then down through the webbing inside the coil (above).

4. Adding more coils.

◆ Place a second spring behind the first, again at the intersection of two webbing strips. At the point where this coil adjoins the first, bring the needle up through the webbing on the inside of the coil (right) and down through the webbing on the outside.

◆ Complete the second and third stitches by pushing the needle up on the inside and down on the outside of the coil; for the fourth stitch, push the needle up on the outside and down on the inside of the coil.

◆ Continue adding and anchoring a spring at each webbing intersection, always placing the new spring next to the last stitch on the previous one (inset). When your stitching takes you into a corner, pass the needle underneath the last stitch; then remove the needle, pull the twine taut, and tie a knot. Begin again by anchoring a new spring in the same way as the first one (Steps 1 and 2).

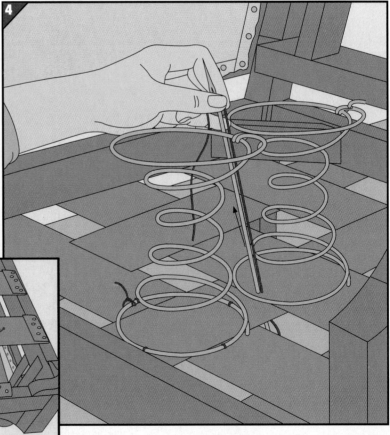

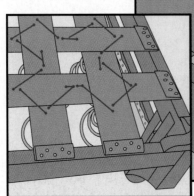

TYING THE COILS TOGETHER

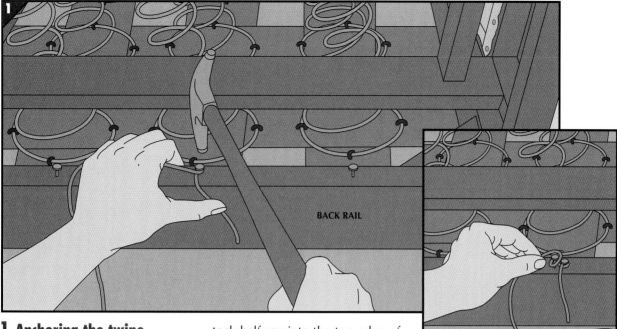

BACK RAIL

1. Anchoring the twine.

◆ For each row of springs, front to back and side to side, cut a length of spring twine 1½ times the distance between the seat rails.

◆ Along each of the four rails and in line with the center of each row of springs, drive a No. 14 tack halfway into the top edge of the frame.

◆ Loop one end of the first length of twine around the middle tack on the back rail and drive the tack all the way into the wood *(above).*

◆ Drive a second tack halfway into the rail ⅛ inch away from the first tack; loop the twine in the opposite direction around this tack, forming a figure 8 *(inset)*. Then drive in the second tack the rest of the way.

2. Tying the coils.

◆ Standing at the front of the frame, draw the anchored twine up under the back brace and under the second coil from the top on the back of the middle-row spring adjacent to the brace.

◆ Compress the spring by about one-third of its height, then pull the twine taut and, while holding it against the coil with your thumb to maintain tension, tie a knot around the coil *(right and inset).*

◆ Draw the twine through the spring, hold it taut against the underside of the top coil, and tie a knot around the top coil.

◆ Working toward the front, tie down the remaining springs in the row by compressing each one and then knotting the twine around the back and front of the top coil.

◆ When you reach the front spring, compress it, then tie one knot at the back of the top coil and another at the front of the second coil from the top.

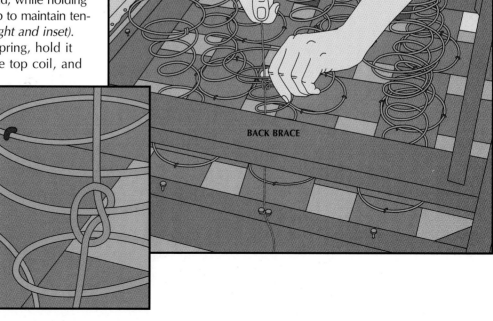

BACK BRACE

3. Securing the twine.

◆ At the front spring, pull the twine tight and loop it on the tack in the rail *(left)*. Drive the tack into the wood, then add a second tack and loop the twine around the tacks in a figure 8 as you did in Step 1.

◆ Tie down the remaining rows of springs on both sides of the middle row in the same fashion, alternating sides.

◆ Tie the side-to-side rows in the same way, again beginning with the middle row and working out to alternate sides, so that each spring is tied with two cords.

4. Tying secondary and diagonal cords.

◆ Drive tacks halfway into the frame around all four sides, midway between those already in place.

◆ For each row of springs, cut a length of spring twine $1\frac{1}{2}$ times the distance between the rails.

◆ Anchor one end of a length of twine to one of the tacks in the back rail as in Step 1, then draw it under the back brace and tie it to each piece of twine it crosses, knotting it as in Step 2 *(right)*. Anchor the end on the opposite rail.

◆ Tie all back-to-front twine in the same way, and then repeat to tie the side-to-side lengths.

◆ Cut twine $1\frac{1}{2}$ times the length of each diagonal row of springs. Starting with the center diagonals and working outward, anchor these lengths to the frame as in Step 1, then tie them to the springs as in Step 2. On the corner springs, tie both knots on the second coil from the top; otherwise tie the first and last knots in each row one coil from the top. Once all the rows in one direction are tied, repeat the procedure with rows running the opposite way *(inset)*.

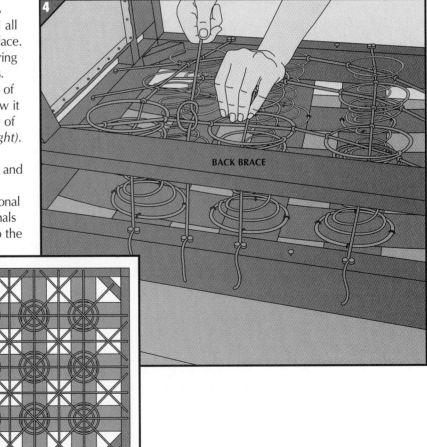

BACK BRACE

FIXING ZIGZAG SPRINGS

Securing the springs.
To secure springs that have slipped out of line:
◆ Cut lengths of spring twine to span the seat, allowing a bit extra for tying knots. Anchor the end of one length to the side seat rail with two tacks *(page 97, Step 1)*.
◆ Stretch the twine across the seat, tying it to each spring *(right)*. Then fasten additional cords every 6 to 8 inches.

To reattach clips that have worked loose from the rails:
◆ With pliers, carefully ease the spring out of its metal clip and let it snap back.
◆ With a claw chisel, remove the tacks anchoring the loose clip. Fill the holes with wood glue; let the glue dry.
◆ Reposition the clip as close as possible to its original position at a spot free of tack holes. Fasten the clip with tacks the same size as the originals, then move the clip at the opposite end of the spring in alignment with its new location.
◆ Slip one end of the spring into its clip; then, stretching the spring with pliers, slip the other end into the opposite clip.

> ⚠️ **CAUTION** Stand clear when releasing a stretched zigzag spring—it will snap back and down with force.

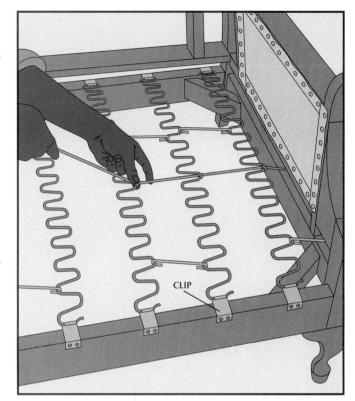

CLIP

REINFORCING A CHAIR BACK

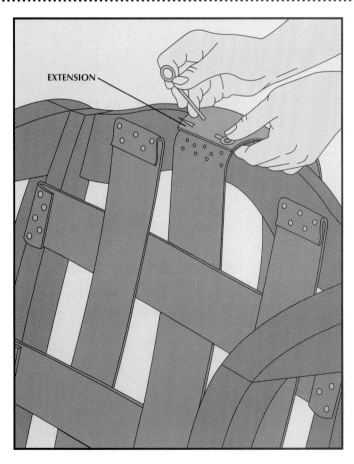

EXTENSION

Tightening the webbing.
◆ With a claw chisel, pry out the tacks holding the top end of the center webbing strip.
◆ Cut an 8-inch length of webbing as an extension and pin it to the original webbing with two upholstery pins, overlapping the strips by 1 inch *(left)*.
◆ Holding a webbing stretcher at a 45-degree angle to the top rail, pull the extension across the top of the rail and onto the teeth of the stretcher; push the stretcher down to a horizontal position *(page 89, Step 2)*.
◆ Holding the stretcher with one hand, retack the original webbing to the inside face of the top rail.
◆ Remove the extension, then stretch the remaining webbing strips on the chair back in the same way.

Over the webbing and springs of a seat, a layer of burlap provides a base for the stuffing. If you have taken a seat apart for rebuilding, you now have to stretch new burlap to cover the springs *(below and opposite)*. If you removed the burlap on the inside back of the chair to expose the webbing, replace this piece as well *(page 102, Step 4)*. Burlap in good shape on the inside arms and wings can be left in place. If it is damaged, however, replace it *(page 102, Step 4)*, using the old piece as a pattern for the new. Loose burlap on an arm or wing can sometimes be tightened *(page 117)*.

As a finishing touch, buy edge roll—a burlap-encased cylinder of either cotton or felt—and tack it along the edge of the front seat rail to pad and shape it. Burlap is also added to the outside of the chair, but only as you fasten on the final fabric cover *(pages 119-120)*.

 TOOLS

Scissors
Tack hammer
Claw chisel or
  staple remover
Curved upholstery
  needle

 MATERIALS

Burlap
Upholstery tacks
  (No. 3)
Nylon stitching
  twine
Edge roll

 **SAFETY TIPS**

Protect your eyes with goggles when removing or hammering tacks.

ADDING A LAYER OF BURLAP

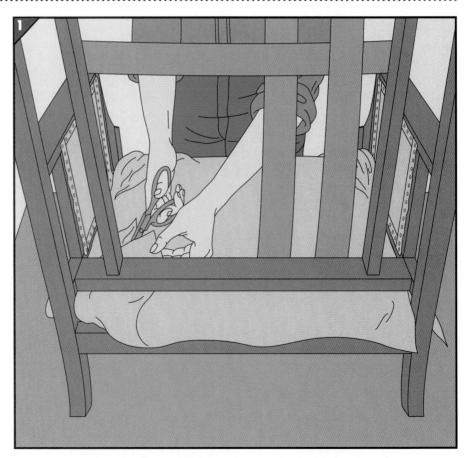

1. Covering the seat springs.
◆ Cut a rectangle of burlap 6 inches longer and wider than the seat frame and center it on the seat. *(Some back webbing has been removed in this illustration for clarity.)*
◆ Fold the extra 3 inches at the back of the chair back toward the center of the seat.
◆ Cut the burlap diagonally from each back corner to the fold so it will fit around the rear legs *(right)*.
◆ Fold back excess material at the front of the chair and cut the burlap to fit around the arm posts.

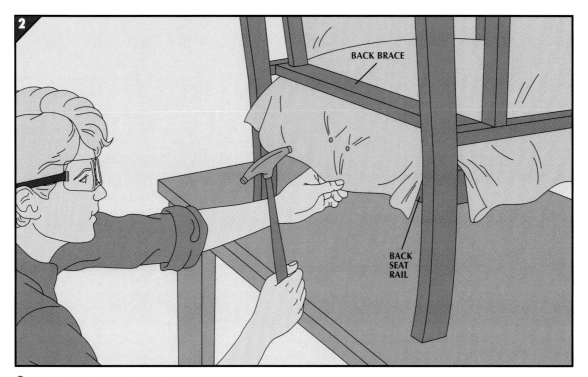

2. Tacking down the edges.

◆ Draw the overlapping edge of burlap down between the back brace and back seat rail and fasten it to the outer face of the rail with No. 3 tacks driven at 2-inch intervals *(above)*.

◆ Pull the burlap taut over the springs and tack it to the center and ends of the front rail. Fill in between the ends with tacks spaced every 2 inches, stretching and smoothing the burlap as you go. Trim the burlap so $\frac{3}{4}$ inch extends past the tacks. Fold over this edge and tack it again.

◆ Stretch and tack the sides in the same way.

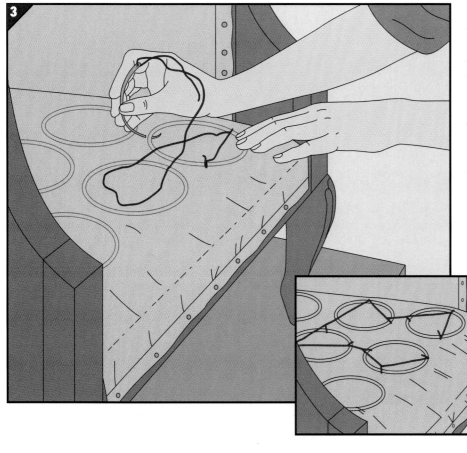

3. Sewing burlap to the springs.

◆ Thread a curved needle with nylon stitching twine.

◆ Starting at a corner spring, locate the first stitch so the third of three evenly spaced stitches will end up near another spring. Push the needle down through the burlap on the outside of the coil and back up inside the coil. Tie a slipknot *(page 95, Step 2)* to anchor the first stitch.

◆ Make two more stitches *(left)*, locking each one by drawing the needle back under the twine from the previous stitch.

◆ Continue sewing the coils one after another *(inset)*. At the end of a length of twine, tie it with a slipknot and continue sewing with a new piece.

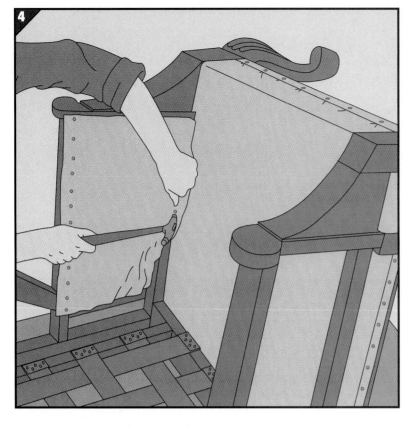

4. Adding burlap to the arms and back.

◆ If the burlap on the inside of the arms is worn or loose, remove it by prying out its fasteners with a claw chisel or staple remover.

◆ Using the old pieces as patterns, cut pieces of burlap to cover the inside of the arms, wings, and back. Make each piece 2 inches larger than the pattern on all sides.

◆ Tack each piece to the inside faces of the frame, starting on one side, then pull the piece taut and tack it on the other side.

◆ Trim away the excess burlap, leaving $\frac{3}{4}$ inch beyond the tacks. Fold over this edge and then tack it again.

CUSHIONING THE FRONT RAIL

Fastening the edge roll.

◆ With sturdy scissors, cut a section of edge roll the same length as the front seat rail.

◆ Holding the roll in position slightly overhanging the edge of the seat, drive No. 14 tacks through its seam allowance and into the front rail, spacing the tacks every 2 inches *(right)*.

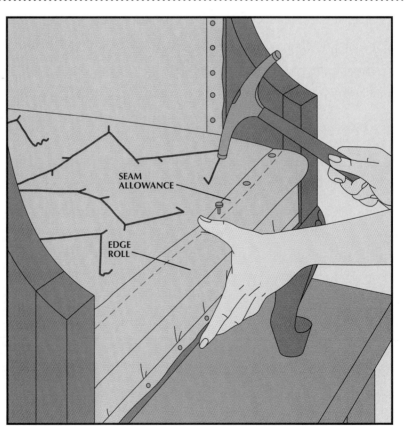

SEAM
ALLOWANCE

EDGE
ROLL

Making the New Cover

Once the chair is ready, you can prepare the fabric for the new cover, using the old pieces as patterns *(below and page 104)*.

Selecting the Fabric: Choose a material that is durable but not too difficult to work with. One of the most popular fabrics is upholstery-weight cotton cloth; look for one that is heavy enough to withstand wear. Almost as strong is spun rayon, but be sure it is labeled "spun rayon" not just "rayon," which wears out too quickly. A cotton/linen blend yields an elegant, lightweight cover. Standard upholstery material—usually a blend of rayon, acetate, nylon, and cotton—is sturdy, but also quite thick and may be difficult to sew. Corduroy will take much punishment, but may be too thick for a home sewing machine. Also difficult to work with are plastics that imitate leather. The decking covering the seat can be made of inexpensive fabric such as cotton denim.

When selecting material for your first project, it's best to avoid patterns with bold designs. Keeping these elements aligned and matched as you cut the pieces and sew them together can be tricky. Whenever possible, buy fabric that has been treated with a dirt-resistant spray, or spray it yourself once you've finished the job.

Sewing the Pieces: Use a sewing machine powerful enough to sew through four layers of material to fashion the welt *(pages 105-106)*. Some machines have a cording attachment for this purpose, but if yours does not, you can use a zipper foot instead. For all stitching you'll need stout thread and needles. The strongest thread is nylon No. 69, 16-gauge, but 4-ply cotton thread (known as 16-4) is adequate. The best needle sizes are 16 or 18. Generally, the density of the fabric calls for a fairly long stitch, 12 or even 8 stitches per inch, but shorten the length around curves and at corners to provide extra strength. You can also stitch each seam twice for additional reinforcement.

TOOLS

Iron
Dressmaker's pins
Scissors
Sewing machine
Straightedge
Marking pencil

MATERIALS

Upholstery fabric
Thread
Welt cord

CUTTING OUT THE MATERIAL

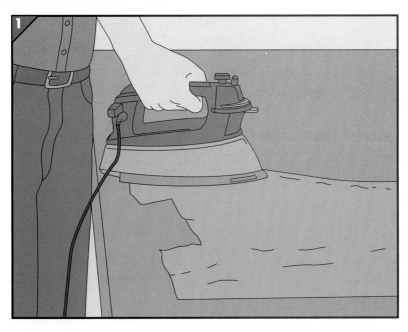

1. Flattening the old fabric.

◆ Place a piece of the old fabric removed from the furniture on a flat surface and smooth it with a steam iron *(left)*. To flatten edges that were folded or joined at seams, run the tip of the iron along the crease.

◆ Turn the fabric over and smooth the other side.

◆ Flatten the remaining pieces in the same fashion.

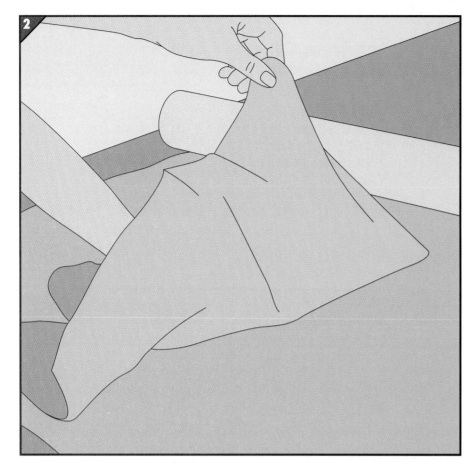

2. Centering the pattern.

◆ Unroll the new upholstery material right side up on the work surface and lay a pattern piece right side up on it *(left)*. Position the pattern piece on the new upholstery so the grain lines of both pieces align. For napped fabrics, orient the pieces so the nap will run down toward the floor when the new upholstery is fastened to the furniture.

◆ Fix the pattern piece to the new fabric with dressmaker's pins placed $\frac{1}{2}$ inch from the edges.

◆ Pin the remaining pieces to the new fabric in the same way, unrolling the upholstery material as you go.

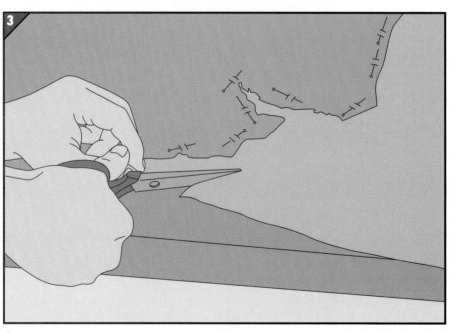

3. Cutting the fabric.

◆ Cut the new fabric pieces from the roll, following the contours of each pattern piece, but adding 2 inches all around to allow for stretching, tacking, and stitching *(above)*. If a pattern piece is torn or missing a corner, cut the new piece a little large to leave room for adjustment when it is attached to the frame.

◆ Mark the top edge of each new piece and label its position on the chair. Then, unpin it from its pattern piece.

JOINING TWO PIECES

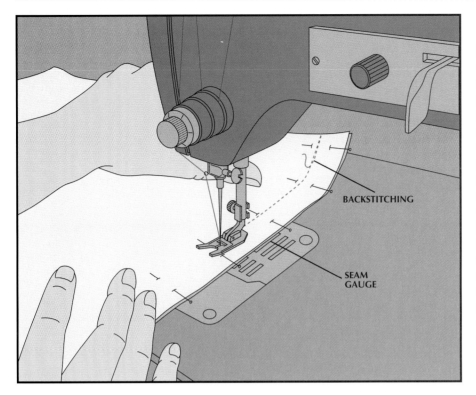

BACKSTITCHING

SEAM GAUGE

Stitching the seams.

◆ Place two pieces of fabric together so their right sides are face to face and the edges to be joined are aligned. Secure the edge with pins placed at right angles to the seam line.

◆ Position the fabric on the sewing machine so the needle is over one corner of the fabric, $\frac{1}{2}$ inch away from the edge and one end.

◆ Set the machine to reverse and stitch backward $\frac{1}{2}$ inch to the end of the fabric, guiding the material by hand along the seam gauge. From this end, stitch forward to the opposite end of the seam (*left*), then backstitch again for about $\frac{1}{2}$ inch.

◆ Stitch the seam a second time for additional strength, if desired.

MAKING WELT

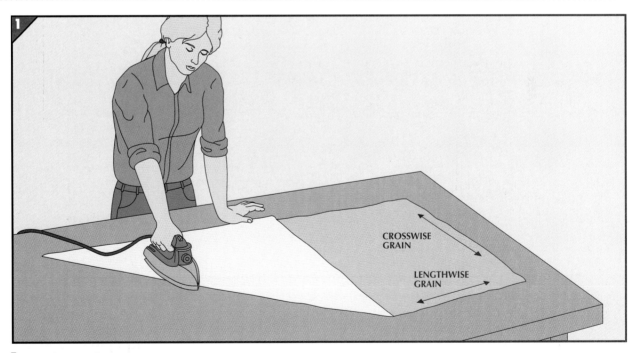

CROSSWISE GRAIN

LENGTHWISE GRAIN

1. Making welt strips.

◆ Set a length of fabric on a flat surface and fold it diagonally so a portion of the fabric's lengthwise grain parallels the crosswise grain.

◆ Press along the diagonal fold with an iron (*above*), then spread open the fabric.

◆ Turn the fabric over. With a straightedge and a marking pencil or tailor's chalk, use the fold line as a guide and draw parallel lines at $1\frac{1}{2}$-inch intervals on the wrong side of the fabric.

◆ Cut along the lines to make the welt strips.

◆ Repeat this process until you have enough strips to make the length of welt you will need when they are joined together.

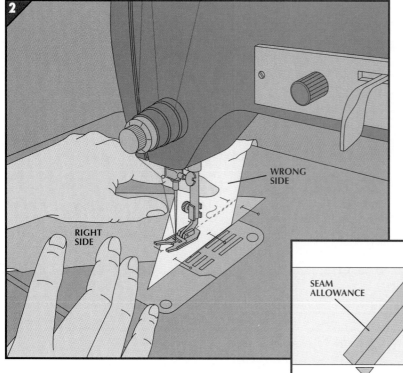

2. Joining strips.

◆ Pin the end of one strip at a 90-degree angle to another with the right sides of the pieces face to face.

◆ Stitch the two pieces together *(left)*, as described on page 105, top. Stitch the seam a second time.

◆ Press the seam open and clip off the corners of the seam allowance that extend beyond the edges of the strips *(inset)*.

◆ Continue joining pieces until you have strips that are as long as the seams to be outlined with welt.

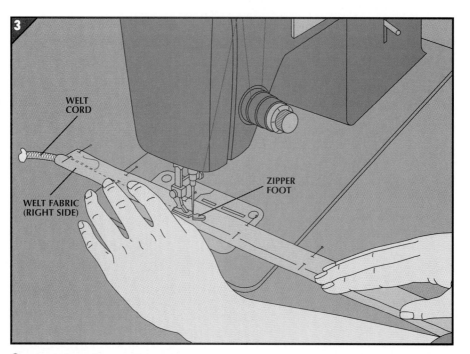

3. Covering the welt cord.

◆ Cut a piece of welt cord 2 inches longer than the fabric strip.

◆ Set the strip wrong side up on a work surface and lay the cord along the middle of the strip with about 1 inch of cord extending beyond each end.

◆ Fold the strip over the cord, align the fabric edges, and pin them together.

◆ If your sewing machine has a cording attachment, follow the manufacturer's instructions to sew the welt. If not, use the zipper foot to sew through the folded fabric, close to but not directly against the cord *(above)*; backstitch for the first $\frac{1}{2}$ inch as you did for the other seams.

◆ If the finished seam allowance is uneven, trim it evenly to $\frac{1}{2}$ inch.

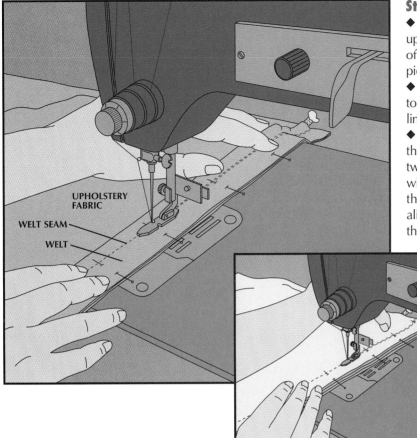

UPHOLSTERY FABRIC

WELT SEAM

WELT

Stitching the welt.

◆ Pin the welt to the right side of the upholstery fabric, keeping the flat edge of the welt and the edge of the fabric piece aligned.

◆ With a zipper foot, stitch the welt to the fabric just inside the welt seam line; backstitch for the first $\frac{1}{2}$ inch *(left)*.

◆ To add a second piece of fabric to the first along the welt edge, pin the two pieces together, right sides facing, with the welt sandwiched between them and the edges of all the layers aligned. Set the assembly down with the first piece on top so the stitching is visible and, using the zipper foot, sew through all the layers of fabric between the existing seam line and the cord *(inset)*.

◆ To reduce the bulk of the seam allowance, trim each layer to a different width, graduating from $\frac{1}{2}$ inch on the bottom layer to $\frac{1}{4}$ inch for the top layer.

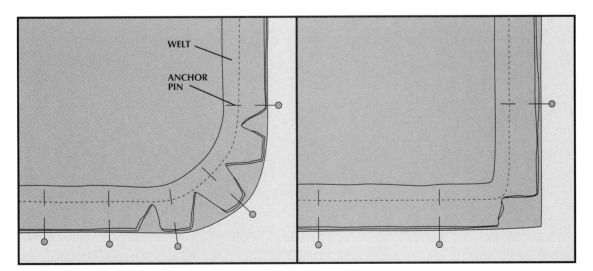

WELT

ANCHOR PIN

Attaching welt around curves and corners.

◆ On a curved seam *(above, left)*, anchor the welt with a pin just short of the curve, keeping the fabric edges aligned.

◆ Pull and pin the welt around the curve, cutting V-shaped notches in the seam allowance of the welt to let the welt lie flat.

◆ With a zipper foot, stitch the welt to the fabric just inside the welt seam line as for a straight seam,

adjusting the sewing machine to shorten the stitch length along the curve.

To turn a sharp corner *(above, right)*, pin the welt to the fabric about 1 inch from the corner.

◆ Notch the seam allowance of the welt at the corner.

◆ Bend the welt around the corner, pin it along the other edge of the fabric, and stitch it in place.

The methods for covering the wing chair shown on these pages can be used on virtually any piece of upholstered furniture. For sofas, the sections of fabric are simply larger. Antiques often have fewer upholstered parts and more exposed wood. Many modern chairs are not really upholstered at all, but covered by cushions screwed to the wood frame—the cushions can be removed and recovered (pages 122-125).

Stuffing and Padding: Where you have stripped the chair frame completely in order to rebuild the seat and back, reuse the stuffing, if it is in good condition, and add a new layer of padding (page 113). If the old materials are still in place, tear off the top layer of padding and add a new one.

Techniques for Fitting and Tacking: During the process of covering the chair, you will be using different techniques to attach the fabric (below and pages 109-112). Where you need to join two pieces of fabric, tack one piece to the frame and fasten the second piece over it. After tacking, trim each piece $\frac{1}{2}$ inch beyond the tacks. Where there is no underlying wood to anchor a joint, however, you need to sew the two pieces together—either by machine before the pieces are tacked down (page 105) or, in some cases, on the chair with blind-stitching. As you fasten the fabric in place, pay special attention to fitting the material around the frame. Upholstery pins come in handy to hold the fabric on vertical sections of the piece while you work.

Covering the Piece: Start by attaching fabric to the inside of the chair (pages 112-118); the raw edges will be hidden by the outside pieces (pages 119-120). Once the cover is in place, you can add decorative buttons and trim, if you wish, to give the piece a different look (page 121). As the job progresses, you'll need to select appropriate fasteners, depending on the number of fabric layers (page 84).

 TOOLS

Tack hammer
Rubber mallet
Scissors
Curved upholstery
  needle

Straight upholstery
  needle (10")
Sewing machine
Upholstery pins
Marking pencil
Tin snips
Glue gun

 **MATERIALS**

Upholstery tacks
  (assorted sizes)
Tack tape
Metal tack strip
Nylon hand-stitching
  thread (No. 18)
Stitching twine

Upholstery fabric
Welt
Decking fabric
Stuffing
Padding
Burlap
Cambric
Gimp
Buttons

 **SAFETY TIPS**

Protect your eyes with goggles when driving tacks.

ANCHORING WITH TACK STRIPS

Blind-tacking a straight line.
With one piece of fabric tacked to the chair frame, fasten the adjoining piece with tack tape.
◆ Position the second, reverse side out, on the chair against the first, aligning the raw edges of the two pieces.
◆ Hold a length of cardboard tack tape along the edge of the pieces, aligned against the welt if there is any, and, with a tack hammer and tacks, fasten the tape to the frame, going through both layers of fabric (right).
◆ Fold the second piece of fabric down over the tack tape.

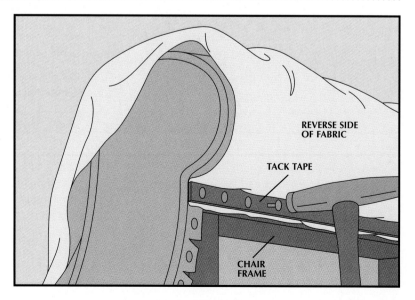

REVERSE SIDE OF FABRIC

TACK TAPE

CHAIR FRAME

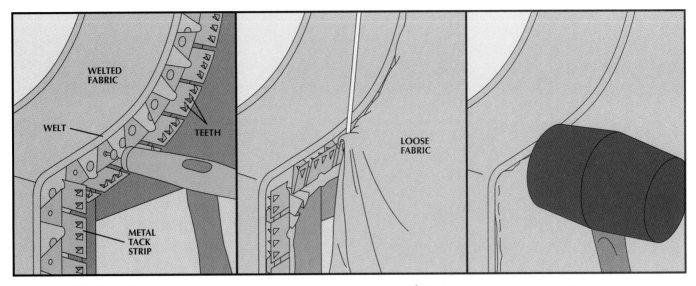

Blind-tacking along a curve.

◆ Position a metal tack strip against the frame, setting the flat side against the seam—or welt, if there is one—with the toothed half of the strip facing out.
◆ Tack the strip to the frame *(above, left)*.
◆ Fold the toothed half up toward the tacked half, leaving a $\frac{1}{4}$-inch gap between them. Tuck the raw edge of the loose fabric into this gap with a 10-inch straight needle *(above, center)*.
◆ Hammer the tack strip shut with a rubber mallet *(above, right)*. The teeth in the strip will hold the fabric in place.

BLIND-STITCHING

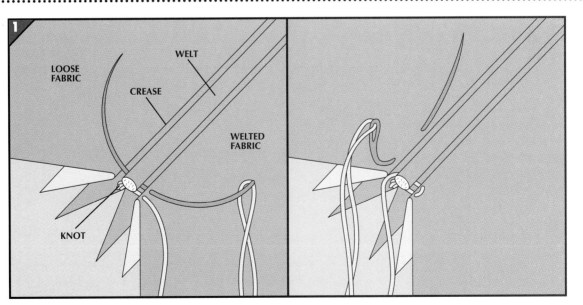

1. Making the first stitch.

◆ Crease the loose fabric $\frac{1}{2}$ inch from the edge.
◆ Cut a length of No. 18 nylon hand-stitching thread twice the length of the seam to be sewn, thread it through a curved upholstery needle, and tie a knot in one end of the thread.
◆ Stitch through the welt close to the cord, bringing the needle up through the welted fabric, then push the needle back through the welted fabric and welt *(above, left)*.
◆ Push the needle down through the top layer of the loose fabric from above; then carry the stitch inside the crease, bringing it up $\frac{1}{2}$ inch farther along *(above, right)*.

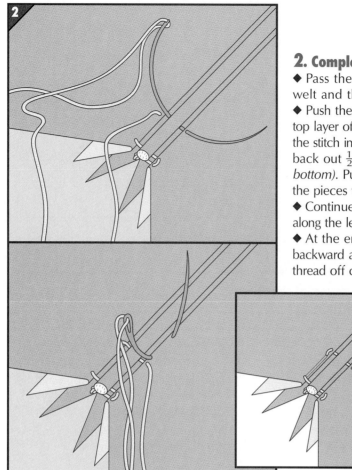

2. Completing the seam.

◆ Pass the needle back through the welt and the welted fabric *(left, top)*.

◆ Push the needle down through the top layer of the welted fabric and carry the stitch inside the crease, bringing it back out $\frac{1}{2}$ inch farther along *(left, bottom)*. Pull the thread tight to draw the pieces together.

◆ Continue stitching in the same way along the length of the seam *(inset)*.

◆ At the end of the seam, blind-stitch backward about 2 inches, then cut the thread off close to the welt.

FITTING AROUND THE FRAME

Slits and pleats for a curve.
To relieve pressure on fabric fitting around an outside curve, cut triangular slits from the edge to within $\frac{1}{4}$ inch of the visible edge. Slit the fabric along the length of the curve at 1-inch intervals.

At an inside curve, fold the fabric edges into $\frac{1}{2}$-inch pleats. To keep pleats even, locate the first one at the middle of the curve and work out toward the ends.

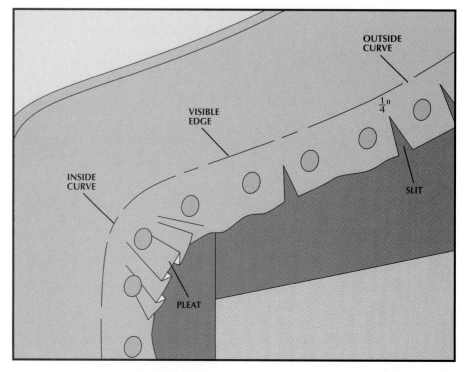

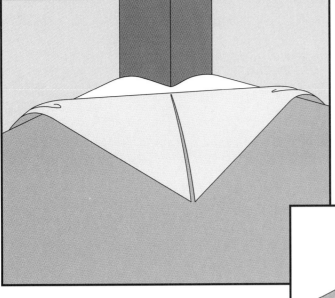

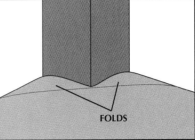

A diagonal cut at corners.

◆ Fold the fabric back diagonally from the corner of the frame part, leaving a narrow gap between the corner and the fold line.

◆ Cut a slit in the fabric from the corner to the fold line *(left)*.

◆ Unfold the fabric and tuck the triangular sections under so they fit against both sides of the frame part *(inset)*.

◆ Secure the fabric to the underside of the frame with tacks.

FOLDS

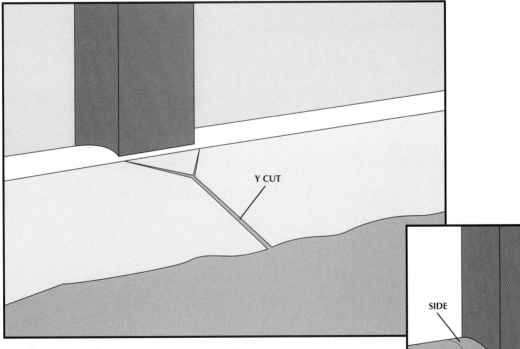

Y CUT

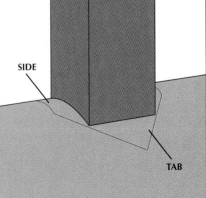

SIDE

TAB

Cutting around a post.

◆ Fold the fabric back, parallel to the edge of the frame, leaving a narrow gap between the fold line and the post.

◆ Cut a Y-shaped slit so the throat of the Y is about 1 inch from the frame and the arms align with the corners of the post *(above)*.

◆ Fold the tab at the top of the Y under, aligning its edge with the inside edge of the frame. Then fold the two sides of the Y under, fitting them neatly against the outer sides of the post *(inset)*.

◆ Tack the bottom edge of the fabric to the underside of the frame.

Tucks around a leg.

◆ Cut into the overhanging fabric at the corners where the leg meets the frame, ending the cuts at the bottom of the frame *(right)*.

◆ Fold the fabric under at the top of the leg and tack the fabric to the underside of the frame *(inset)*.

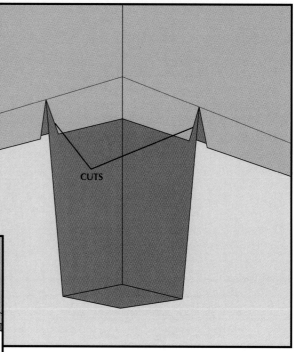

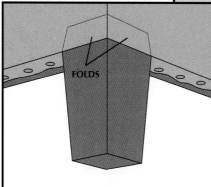

COVERING THE INSIDE OF THE CHAIR

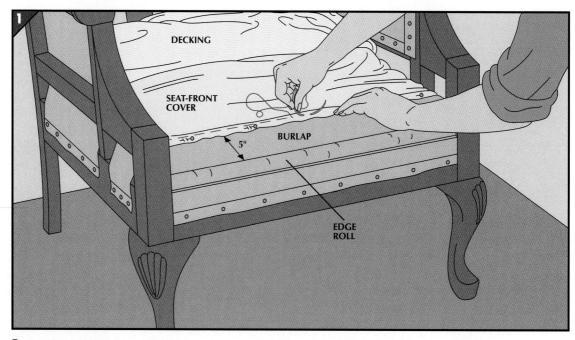

1. Sewing decking to the seat.

◆ Machine-stitch the decking to the seat-front cover *(page 105)*.

◆ Position the seam 5 inches behind the edge roll and pin the decking to the burlap with upholstery pins.

◆ Fold back the seat-front cover to expose the seam allowance. Then thread a curved upholstery needle with stitching twine and sew the seam allowance to the burlap with 1-inch-long stitches *(above)*; place the stitches as close as possible to the seam.

2. Stitching down stuffing.

◆ Fold the seat-front cover and decking down over the front of the chair.

◆ Replace the old stuffing or cut a piece of stuffing to fit the area within the side and back seat rails and the seam line between the decking and the burlap.

◆ Thread a curved upholstery needle with stitching twine and guide it down through the stuffing and burlap and under the top coil of the underlying spring.

◆ Work around the perimeter of the stuffing, making one stitch per spring *(right)*.

◆ Cut stuffing for the inside back, arms, and wings, shaping each piece to fit between the inside edges of the frame. Stitch the stuffing to the burlap.

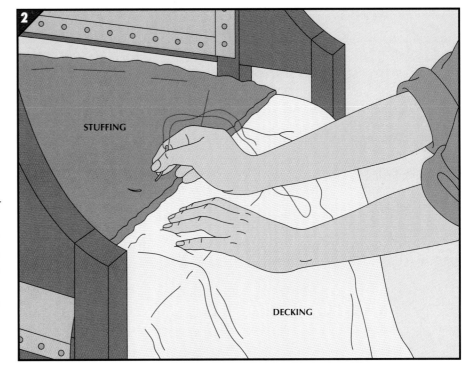

STUFFING

DECKING

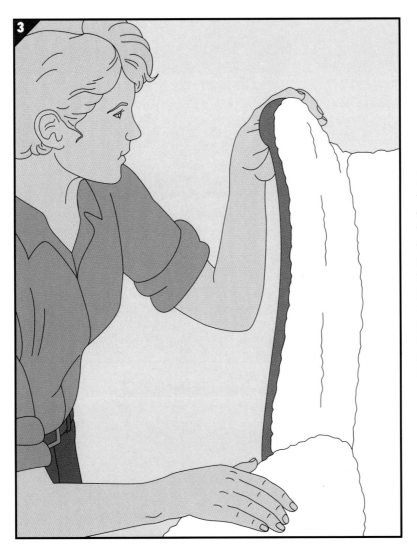

3. Adding padding.

◆ If the old padding is still in place, tear off the top layer.

◆ Place a piece of new padding over each inside surface of the arms, backs, and wings, forming each one roughly to the shape of the chair. Butt adjoining pieces together, but leave space for upholstery fabric to be pushed between pieces to the outside of the chair.

◆ Add a piece of padding to cover the seat stuffing, leaving the front part of the seat bare for now.

4. Tacking the decking.

◆ Fold the decking back over the stuffing and slit its rear corners to fit it around the back stiles of the chair frame *(page 111)*.

◆ Pull the decking through the back and sides of the frame—between the seat and the back and arm braces.

◆ Holding the decking taut, anchor it loosely to the middles of the back seat rail and each side seat rail with upholstery tacks driven halfway in *(right)*.

◆ Working from the middle to the end of each rail, tack the decking to the rails at 1-inch intervals, driving all the fasteners in fully.

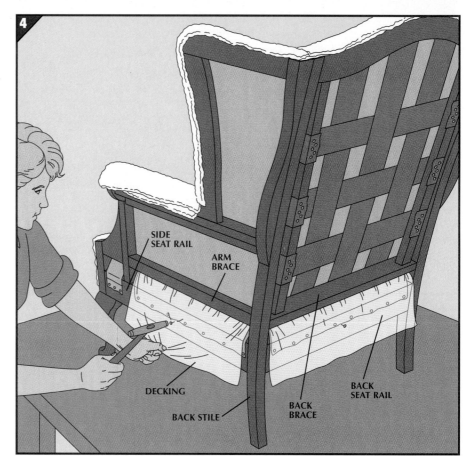

SIDE SEAT RAIL

ARM BRACE

DECKING

BACK STILE

BACK BRACE

BACK SEAT RAIL

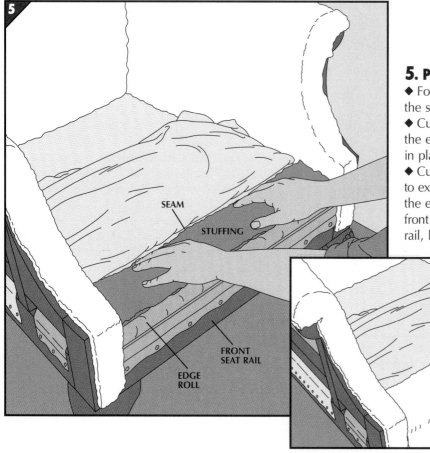

SEAM

STUFFING

FRONT SEAT RAIL

EDGE ROLL

5. Padding the seat front.

◆ Fold back the seat-front cover along the seam line.

◆ Cut a piece of stuffing to fit between the edge roll and the seam, and set it in place *(left)*.

◆ Cut a piece of padding large enough to extend from the seam and down over the edge roll to the bottom edge of the front seat rail. Tack the padding to the rail, leaving it free along the top *(inset)*.

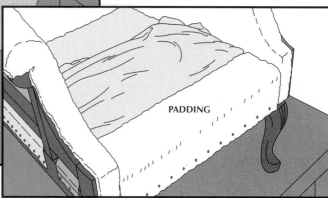

PADDING

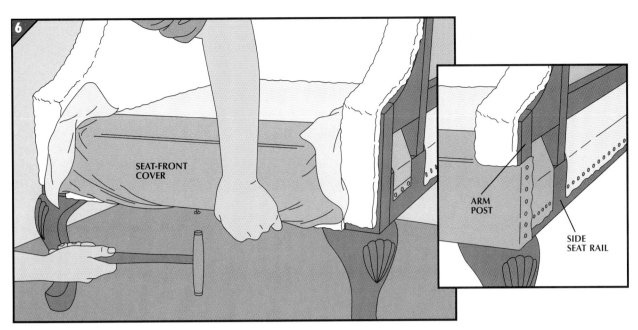

6. Covering the front seat rail.

◆ Pull the seat-front cover down over the padding; hold it taut and tack it loosely to the underside of the front seat rail *(above)*.

◆ Slit the sides of the cover to fit around the arm posts *(page 111)*, and secure it to the outside of the arm posts and to the side seat rails with a half-driven tack.

◆ Cut and fold the cover so it fits neatly around the front legs *(page 112, top)*, and fasten it to the underside of the front seat rail and to the arm posts and side seat rails, driving the tacks all the way in *(inset)*.

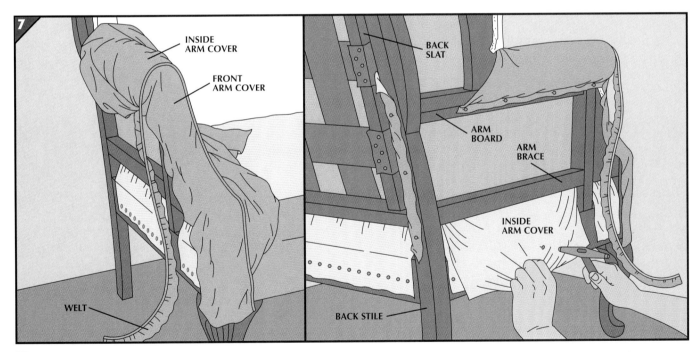

7. Covering the inside arm.

◆ Cut a piece of welt long enough to encircle the front arm cover.

◆ Machine-stitch an inside arm cover to the inside edge of the front arm cover with the welt sandwiched between the two *(page 107)*; do not sew the welt to the outside of the front arm cover.

◆ Place the joined pieces on the chair

and pull the top of the inside arm cover over the arm *(above, left)*; tack it loosely to the outside of the arm board.

◆ Pull the back edge of the inside arm cover through the gap between the back slat and the back stile, and tack it loosely to the back stile.

◆ Slit the bottom edge of the cover to fit around the arm post *(page 111)*, pull

the fabric through the gap between the seat and the arm brace, and tack it loosely to the outside of the side seat rail *(above, right)*.

◆ Adjust the cover to fit smoothly over the arm padding, slitting it at the edges to eliminate wrinkles and bunching.

◆ Fasten the cover to the arm board, back stile, and side seat rail, driving the tacks all the way in at 1-inch intervals.

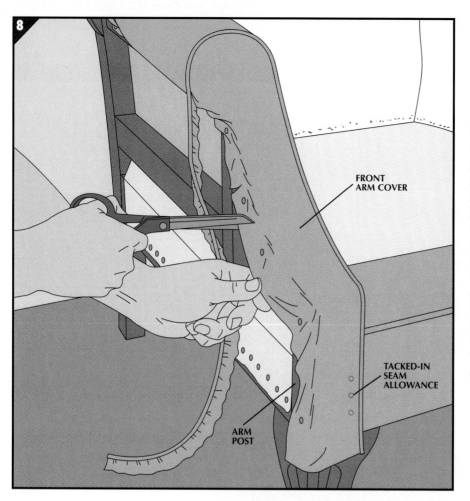

FRONT ARM COVER

TACKED-IN SEAM ALLOWANCE

ARM POST

8. Fitting the front arm cover.
◆ Fold back the front arm cover and fasten the bottom of the welted seam allowance to the arm post with three tacks; drive the last tack about 1 inch above the top of the chair leg.
◆ Draw the cover tightly over the stuffing, tacking it loosely to the outside of the arm post to hold it in place.
◆ Following the technique described on page 110, snip and pleat the fabric to fit neatly around the curve of the arm *(left)*.
◆ Tack the cover to the post at about 1-inch intervals, stopping 1 inch short of the top of the chair leg.

9. Fastening the arm welt.
◆ Hold the loose end of the welt against the curve of the front arm cover. Tack the welt to the outside of the arm post *(right)*, clipping and pleating it as necessary for a neat fit; stop 1 inch from the top of the chair leg.
◆ Along the sharp curve at the top of the arm, blind-stitch *(pages 109-110)* the loose part of the inside arm cover to the welt of the front arm.

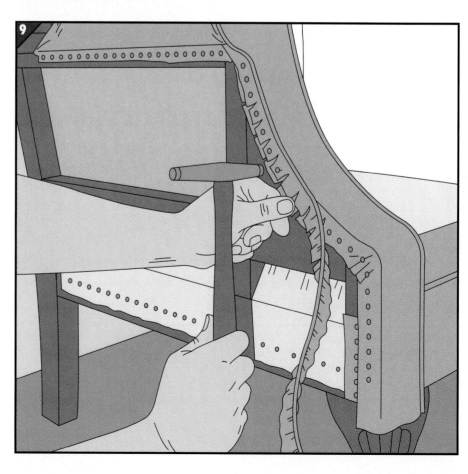

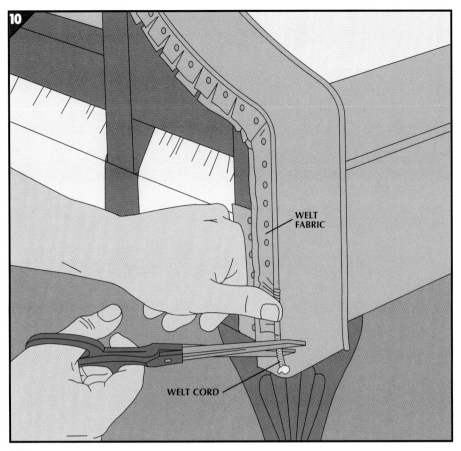

10. Finishing the end of the welt.

◆ Grasp the end of the cord at one end of the welt and retract the fabric to expose more of the cord. Snip off the end of the cord even with the top of the chair leg (*above*) and pull the excess fabric back over the end. Cut the other end of the welt cord the same way.

◆ Fold the fabric under, even with the top of the leg, and tack it to the arm post just above the leg with decorative tacks. Alternatively, if the legs are removable, you can take them off and tack the fabric to the bottom of the chair.

Repeat Steps 7 to 10 to cover the other arm.

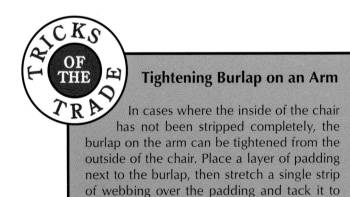

Tightening Burlap on an Arm

In cases where the inside of the chair has not been stripped completely, the burlap on the arm can be tightened from the outside of the chair. Place a layer of padding next to the burlap, then stretch a single strip of webbing over the padding and tack it to the frame (*right*).

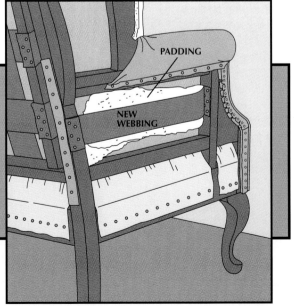

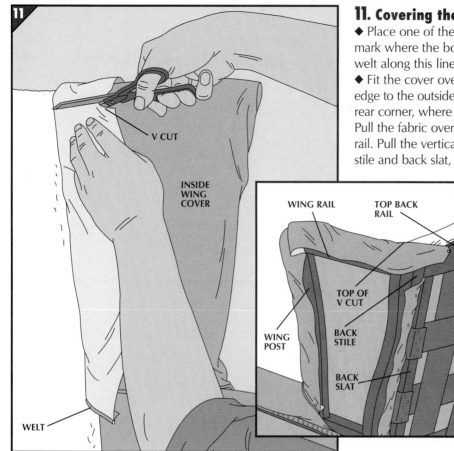

V CUT

INSIDE WING COVER

WELT

11. Covering the inside wing.

◆ Place one of the inside wing covers against a wing and mark where the bottom of the cover meets the arm. Attach welt along this line *(page 107)*.

◆ Fit the cover over the wing, loosely tacking the bottom edge to the outside of the wing frame. Make a V cut at the top rear corner, where the top back rail meets the back stile *(left)*. Pull the fabric over the top back rail and tack it loosely to the rail. Pull the vertical edge through the gap between the back stile and back slat, and tack it loosely to the back stile *(inset)*.

WING RAIL   **TOP BACK RAIL**

TOP OF V CUT

WING POST   **BACK STILE**

BACK SLAT

◆ Lap the fabric over the wing and, holding it taut, pleat it to fit around the sharp curve along the front of the wing top *(page 110)*; drive tacks all the way through the pleats into the top wing rail and into the wing post.

◆ Slit the fabric to fit along the gentler curves at the top and front of the wing and tack it in place loosely. Smooth the fabric and drive tacks all the way into the front, back, and top of the wing frame at 1-inch intervals.

◆ Blind-stitch the welted bottom edge to the inside arm *(pages 109-110)*.

◆ Cover the other inside wing in the same way.

12. Covering the inside back.

◆ Lay the inside back cover in place.

◆ Make a V cut at each top corner where the top back rail meets the back stile *(right)*, and one more at each bottom corner where the back stile meets the back brace.

◆ Pull the cover taut over the top of the back and through the gaps in the sides and bottom of the frame *(inset)*.

◆ Tack the cover loosely to the outside of the top back rail.

◆ Pull the sides of the cover over the back stiles and tack them loosely to the stiles.

◆ Pull the bottom edge downward and tack it loosely to the back seat rail.

◆ Starting from the midpoint of each stile or rail, secure the cover to the frame with tacks driven in all the way at 1-inch intervals.

Attach buttons to the back, if desired *(page 121)*.

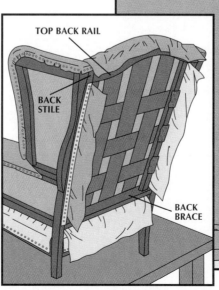

TOP BACK RAIL

BACK STILE

BACK BRACE

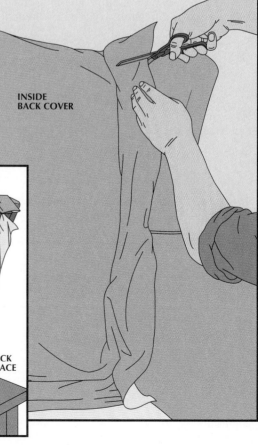

INSIDE BACK COVER

FASTENING THE OUTSIDE COVER

1. Tacking on the welt.

◆ Cut a length of welt to fit along the outer edge of the two wings and the back, adding 2 inches at the ends.

◆ Tack one end of the welt to the arm board just below the wing.

◆ Fasten the welt along the edge of the wings and back, driving tacks at 1-inch intervals *(right)*; clip or pleat the welt's seam allowance, as needed, to fit around curves *(page 110)*.

◆ Tack the other end of the welt to the opposite arm board.

◆ Slide back the fabric at each end of the welt and clip the cord in line with the top of the arm board.

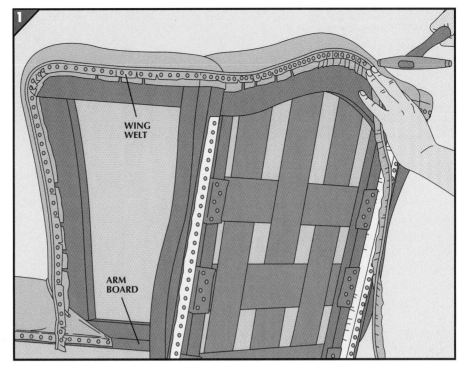

WING WELT

ARM BOARD

2. Attaching the outside wing cover.

◆ Fasten a length of metal tack strip to the outside of the wing frame, beginning at the bottom of the wing post and following the line of the wing welt. Stop at the upper rear corner of the wing *(left)*.

◆ Tack a piece of burlap to the wing frame, trim the burlap $\frac{3}{4}$ inch beyond the tacks, and tack it again to keep it from tearing. Tack a layer of cotton padding over the burlap.

◆ Place the outside wing cover over the wing, and tack it loosely to the rear of the back stile and to the arm board.

◆ Blind-tack the cover to the frame at the front and top of the wing *(page 109)*. Then fasten it directly to the frame along the back and bottom of the wing *(inset)*, driving tacks at 1-inch intervals.

◆ Attach the opposite outside wing cover in the same way.

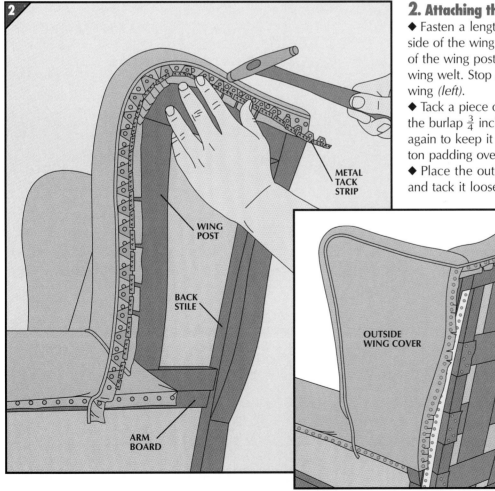

METAL TACK STRIP

WING POST

BACK STILE

ARM BOARD

OUTSIDE WING COVER

3. Fitting the outside arm cover.

◆ Turn the chair on its side and fasten a metal tack strip to the arm post along the welt outlining the front of the outside arm *(right)*.

◆ Tack burlap over the outside arm and a layer of cotton padding over it.

◆ Place the outside arm cover wrong side out on top of the arm, aligning the top edge with the edge of the inside arm cover.

◆ With cardboard tack tape, blind-tack the outside arm cover in place *(page 108)*, driving the tacks into the arm board *(inset)*.

◆ Fold the arm cover back over the arm and loosely tack the back edge to the rear of the back stile and the bottom edge to the bottom of the side seat rail.

◆ Blind-tack the front edge in the tack strip against the welt *(page 109)*.

◆ Cut and fold the bottom edge of the cover to fit around the front and back legs *(page 112)*.

◆ Fasten the back and bottom edges with tacks driven all the way at 1-inch intervals.

◆ Repeat the procedure to cover the other outside arm.

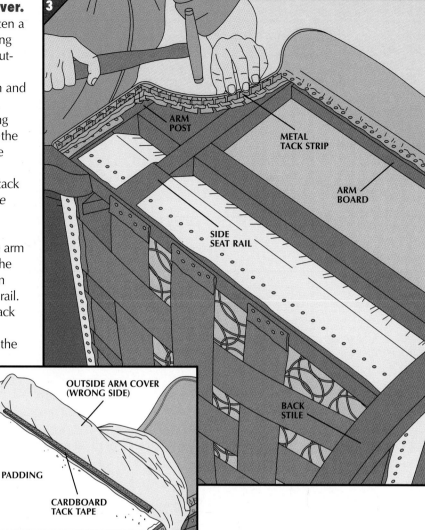

ARM POST

METAL TACK STRIP

ARM BOARD

SIDE SEAT RAIL

BACK STILE

OUTSIDE ARM COVER (WRONG SIDE)

PADDING

CARDBOARD TACK TAPE

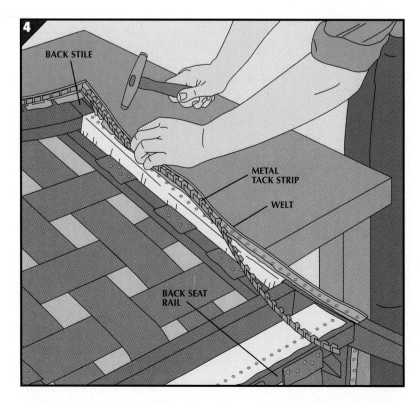

BACK STILE

METAL TACK STRIP

WELT

BACK SEAT RAIL

4. Covering the outside back.

◆ Turn the chair so its back is horizontal, tack strips of welt down the full length of each side of the back, and finish the ends of the welt at both top and bottom *(page 117, Step 10)*.

◆ Outline the top and sides of the back with a continuous length of metal tack strip *(left)*.

◆ Tack burlap over the back, then tack a layer of cotton padding over the burlap.

◆ Using the metal tacking strip, blind-tack the back cover to the back *(page 109)*.

◆ Tack the bottom edge of the cover to the underside of the back seat rail at 1-inch intervals, folding and fitting the cover at the rear legs *(page 112)*.

◆ Cover the bottom of the chair with cambric *(page 90)*.

Hiding a raw edge.

You can conceal any tacks securing fabric to the outside of a chair frame with gimp—ornamental trim—with decorative tacks, or with both.

◆ For gimp, cut a piece long enough to outline the bottom of the chair.

◆ With a glue gun, apply a bead of glue 10 inches long to the edge of the fabric, then press the gimp into the glue, smoothing it with your hand. Continue gluing the gimp to the chair in 10-inch sections *(right)*.

◆ For an additional decorative touch, you can tap broad-headed decorative tacks through the gimp *(inset)*.

To hide exposed tacks with decorative tacks, cover the edge with a continuous row of them, heads touching.

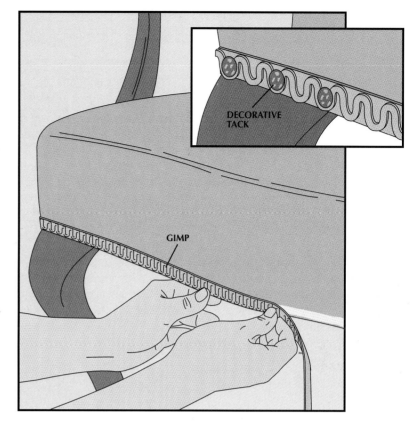

Attaching decorative buttons.

Buttons are fastened to the inside back cover before the outside cover is attached.

◆ Mark locations for the buttons on the inside back cover.

◆ For each button, cut a length of nylon stitching twine about 18 inches long, and thread the twine through the eye on the back of the button. Then bring the two ends of the twine together and thread them through the eye of a 10-inch straight needle.

◆ Push the needle through the inside cover of the chair back at one of the marks *(left)*, and pull it through to the outside.

◆ From the rear, fasten the button twine to the webbing of the chair back with a knot made with the two ends of the twine, inserting a wad of cotton padding into the knot before tightening it. Secure the twine with two additional knots.

◆ Follow the same procedure to sew on the remaining buttons.

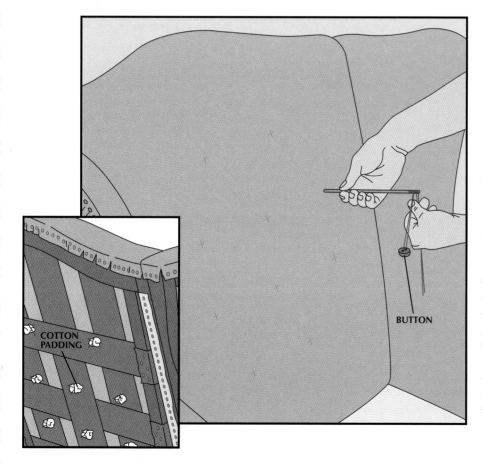

Loose seat cushions commonly consist of stuffing encased in fabric *(below)*. The stuffing in modern cushions is usually foam, but older cushions may be filled with rubberized hair, moss, or tow; some even contain springs. In expensive furniture, the cushion may be filled with down encased in an inner cover of down-proof ticking.

Reviving a Down Cushion: You can fluff up matted down by hanging the cushion on a clothesline and beating it with a broom. Or, tumble the cushion—along with a clean sneaker or tennis balls—in a clothes dryer on low heat. You can also try adding more down to the cushion with a funnel. If the down needs to be replaced, it's best to entrust the job to a professional.

Replacing the Cover: With a seam ripper or a craft knife, carefully open the seams of the old cushion cover. Use the material from the top and bottom as patterns for the new pieces *(pages 103-104)*.

For the boxing—the fabric around the edges of the cushion—cut strips of upholstery fabric along the lengthwise grain of the material. Cut strips 1 inch wider than the height of the cushion, trimming one strip as long as the combined length of the front and sides, and two more strips 8 inches longer than the back.

Stuffing: If you are covering an old cushion, you may want to discard the stuffing and springs, and substitute a slab of foam. Polyurethane foam (or polyfoam) is available in several grades—denser and heavier foam lasts longer. Polyfoam with a density of 1.5 pounds per cubic foot and a compressibility of 35 pounds is ideal. If you are using foam rubber, choose a medium density.

If possible, have your supplier cut the foam to the desired size—standard cushion thicknesses are 3 and 4 inches. To round the contours of a cushion, add a layer of polyester padding to the top and bottom of the foam. Padding can also be used to fill out the contours of an old cushion.

 **TOOLS**

Scissors
Dressmaker's pins
Seam ripper
Sewing machine
Electric
 carving knife

 **MATERIALS**

Upholstery fabric
Welt
Upholstery zipper
Foam stuffing
Polyester batting
Aerosol adhesive

Anatomy of a box cushion.

In the cushion at right, the front boxing strip is cut into three pieces—one 5 inches longer than the cushion front, and two even lengths for the sides. The two back boxing strips are folded in half lengthwise, right side out, and the open edges are stitched together, creating two double-thick back strips to hold the zipper along the folds. The edges of the cushion are outlined with welt cut 2 inches longer than the perimeter of the cushion.

WELT

FRONT BOXING

SIDE BOXING

BACK BOXING

OUTLINING WITH WELT

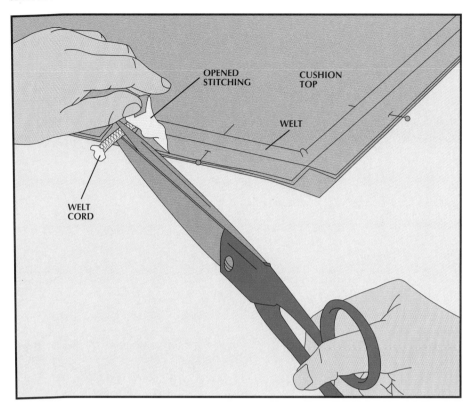

OPENED STITCHING

CUSHION TOP

WELT

WELT CORD

Joining welt ends.

◆ Cut welt 2 inches longer than the perimeter of the cushion.

◆ Starting at the center back of the cushion top, with the fabric right side up, pin the welt around the piece; clip a square section from the welt fabric at the corners so that it lies flat.

◆ Open the stitching at one end of the welt and cut the exposed cord *(left)* so it butts against the covered cord at the other end of the welt.

◆ Trim the opened welt cover $\frac{1}{2}$ inch longer than the exposed cord, fold $\frac{1}{4}$ inch of the fabric, and lap it over the other end of the welt. Pin the joint to the cushion top.

◆ Sew the welt in place with a zipper foot *(page 107)*.

◆ Repeat this procedure for the cushion bottom.

INSTALLING A ZIPPER

1. Sewing in the zipper.

◆ Fold a back boxing strip in half, right side out, and sew the halves together $\frac{1}{4}$ inch from the open edges. Repeat the procedure for the other back strip.

◆ Set the zipper tape on a work surface and position the back boxing strips so one end of both strips lines up with the top of the tape, and the folded edges of the strips are touching. Pin the zipper tape in place.

◆ Open the zipper partway and, starting at its top end, stitch the tape to one boxing strip, $\frac{1}{4}$ inch from the folded edge *(right)*. When you reach the glider, close the zipper.

◆ At the base, pivot and stitch across the zipper tape.

◆ Pivot again and stitch along the other folded edge, $\frac{1}{4}$ inch from the fold. When you reach the bottom of the glider, open the zipper.

◆ Make the last few stitches to the top, then close the zipper completely, pivot, and stitch across the top, just above the glider.

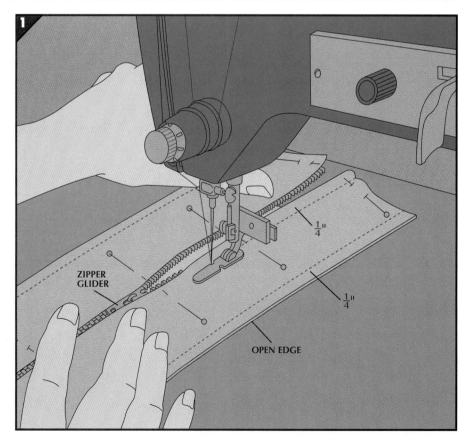

1

$\frac{1}{4}$"

$\frac{1}{4}$"

ZIPPER GLIDER

OPEN EDGE

2. Attaching the side boxing.

◆ Pin a piece of side boxing to the end of the back boxing where the zipper glider is located, right sides together *(right, top)*.

◆ Stitch a seam to join these pieces ½ inch from the end of the strips.

◆ With the fabric right side up, fold 2 inches of the side boxing over the end of the zipper, creating a pocket to hide the glider *(right, bottom)*. Pin the pocket edges to the back boxing and stitch them to the back boxing ½ inch from each edge of the strip.

◆ Pin the second piece of side boxing to the other end of the back boxing, right sides together, and stitch a seam ½ inch from the end of the strips.

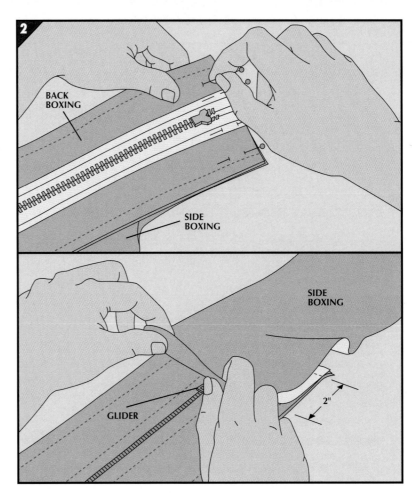

ASSEMBLING THE CUSHION

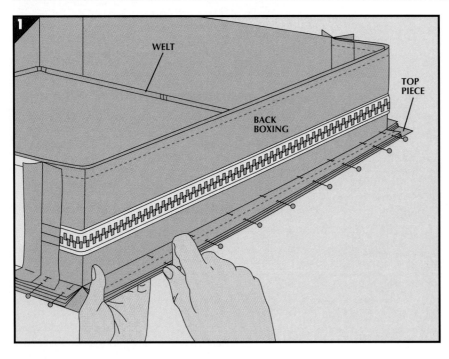

1. Pinning boxing to the cushion top.

◆ Mark the centers of the back boxing strip and the cushion top, and align the marks, with the right sides of the fabric together. Starting from the marks, pin the pieces together, clipping the boxing at the corners to ensure a smooth fit.

◆ Mark the centers of the front boxing strip and the cushion top and pin them together in the same way as for the back boxing strip.

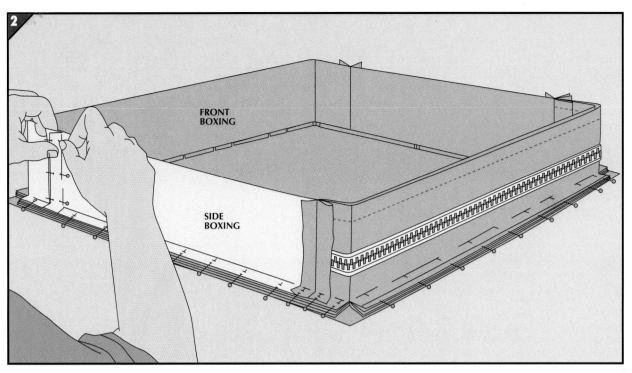

2. Joining the front and side boxing.

◆ Pin one end of the front boxing strip to one of the side boxing strips, then pin the remaining ends, taking up in the seam any excess boxing fabric so it fits smoothly around the cushion top *(above)*.

◆ Stitch both seams to join the boxing strips, and sew the boxing fabric to the cushion top $\frac{1}{2}$ inch from the edges.
◆ Open the zipper, then pin the boxing to the bottom piece, good sides together. Sew the pieces together $\frac{1}{2}$ inch from the edges, then turn the cushion cover right side out.

PUTTING IN THE STUFFING

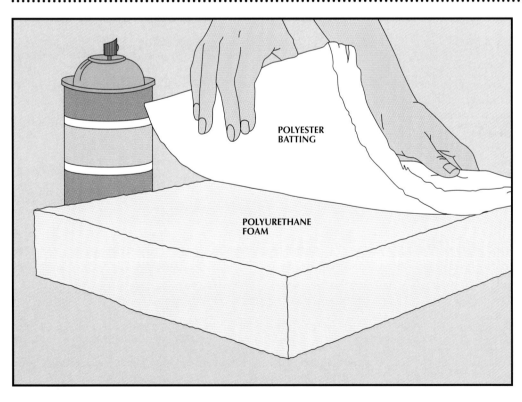

POLYESTER BATTING

POLYURETHANE FOAM

Rounding the contours.

◆ With an electric carving knife or a serrated bread knife, cut the foam to size.
◆ Spray the top of the foam with an aerosol adhesive suitable for polyurethane foam or foam rubber.
◆ Lay a sheet of polyester batting on top of the foam, press it in place, and trim it with scissors to fit the cushion cover. Add batting to the bottom.
◆ Slide the cushion into the cover, compressing the foam and reaching inside to push it into the corners.
◆ Close the zipper.

INDEX

TIME® LIFE BOOKS

Time-Life Books is a division of Time Life Inc.

TIME LIFE INC.
PRESIDENT and CEO: George Artandi

TIME-LIFE BOOKS
PRESIDENT: John D. Hall
PUBLISHER/MANAGING EDITOR:
Neil Kagan

HOME REPAIR AND IMPROVEMENT:
Repairing Furniture
EDITOR: Lee Hassig
MARKETING DIRECTOR: James Gillespie
Art Director: Kathleen Mallow
Associate Editor/Research and Writing:
  Karen Sweet
Marketing Manager: Wells Spence

Vice President, Director of Finance:
  Christopher Hearing
Vice President, Book Production:
  Marjann Caldwell
Director of Operations: Betsi McGrath
Director of Photography and Research:
  John Conrad Weiser
Director of Editorial Administration:
  Barbara Levitt
Production Manager: Marlene Zack
Quality Assurance Manager: James King
Library: Louise D. Forstall

ST. REMY MULTIMEDIA INC.
President and Chief Executive Officer:
  Fernand Lecoq
President and Chief Operating Officer:
  Pierre Léveillé
Vice President, Finance: Natalie Watanabe
Managing Editor: Carolyn Jackson
Managing Art Director: Diane Denoncourt
Production Manager: Michelle Turbide

Staff for Repairing Furniture

Series Editors: Marc Cassini, Heather Mills
Art Director: Michel Giguère
Assistant Editor: Rebecca Smollett
Designers: Jean-Guy Doiron, Robert Labelle
Editorial Assistant: James Piecowye
Coordinator: Dominique Gagné
Copy Editor: Judy Yelon
Indexer: Linda Cardella Cournoyer
Systems Coordinator: Éric Beaulieu
Other Staff: Linda Castle, Lorraine Doré

PICTURE CREDITS
Cover: Photograph, Robert Chartier.
  Art, Maryo Proulx. Chair made by Giles
  Miller-Mead.

Illustrators: Jack Arthur, Gilles Beauchemin,
  Frederic F. Bigio from B-C Graphics, Laszlo
  Bodrogi, François Daxhelet, Roger C.
  Essley, Charles Forsythe, Forte Inc., William
  J. Hennessy Jr., Elsie J. Hennig, Walter
  Hilmers Jr. from HJ Commercial Art,
  Dick Lee, John Martinez, John Massey,
  Joan S. McGurren, Eduino J. Pereira,
  Jacques Perrault, Melissa B. Pooré,
  Snowden Associates, W. F. McWilliam

Photographers: **End papers:** Glenn Moores
  and Chantal Lamarre. **13, 14, 20, 22, 24,
  28, 34, 41, 44, 53, 57, 69, 71, 72, 75,
  79, 81, 86, 94:** Robert Chartier.

ACKNOWLEDGMENTS
The editors wish to thank the following indi-
viduals and institutions: American Tool
Companies Inc., Kenosha, WI; Cone Uphol-
stery, St. Paul, MN; Connecticut Cane &
Reed Co., Manchester, MN; Elmer's Prod-
ucts Inc., Columbus, OH; J. Ennis Fabrics
Ltd., Edmonton, Alberta; Louis V. Genuario,
Genuario Construction Company, Inc.,
Alexandria, VA; Inter Mares Trading Co.,
Lindenhurst, NY; Chris Minick, Stillwater,
MN; Mohawk Products of Canada, St-
Leonard, Quebec; C.S. Osborne & Co.,
Harrison, NJ; Quality Upholstery Supplies
Inc., Montreal, Quebec; St. Urbain Uphol-
stery, Montreal, Quebec; Swing Paints
Limited, Montreal, Quebec; Upholstery
Unlimited, Hudson, NY; Woodcraft Supply
Corp., Parkersburg, WV

Library of Congress
Cataloging-in-Publication Data
Repairing Furniture / by the editors of
  Time-Life Books.
p. cm. — (Home repair and improvement)
Includes index.
ISBN 0-7835-3910-X
1. Furniture — Repairing. 2. Furniture
  Finishing.
I. Time-Life Books. II. Series.
TT199.R467   1997
684.1'044 — DC21   97-1232